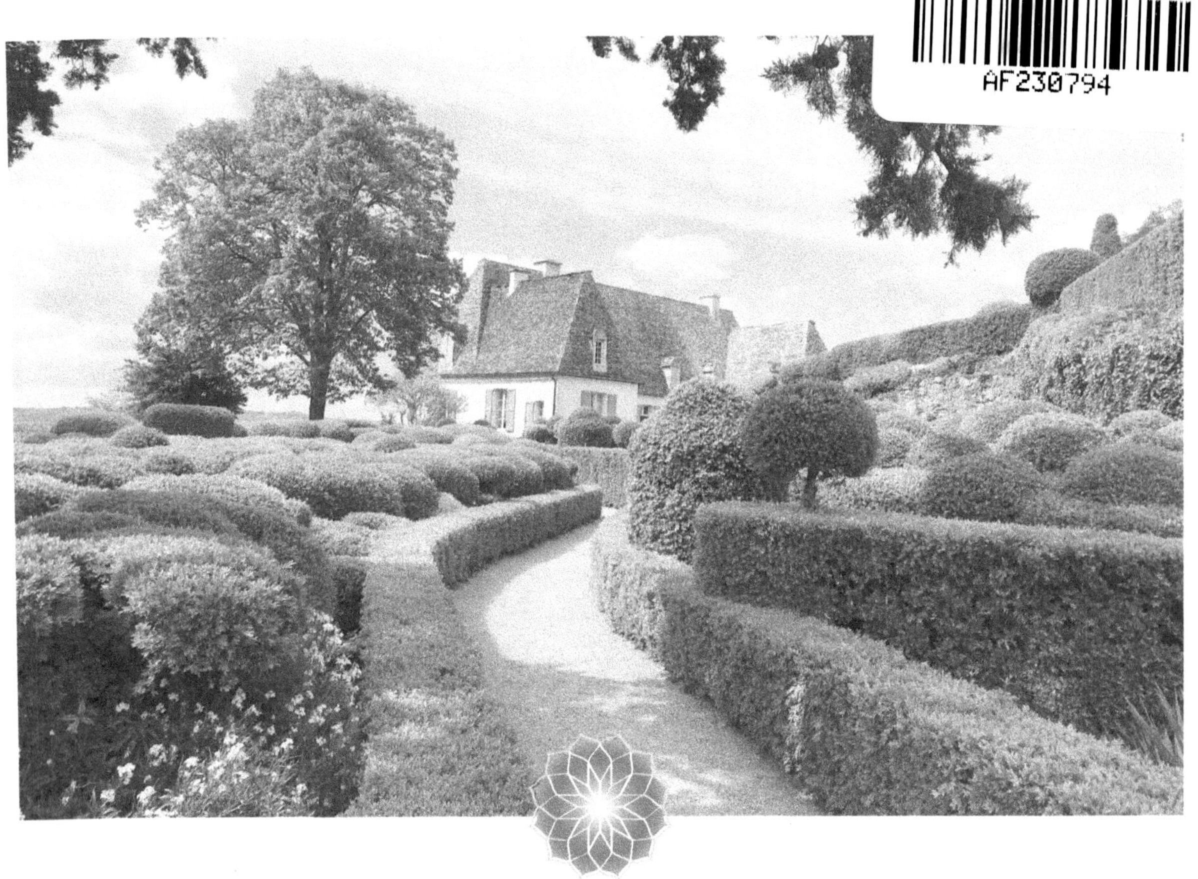

TURN YOUR WORLD UPSIDE DOWN TO GET YOUR LIFE RIGHT SIDE UP

Reverse Thinking Based on *A Course in Miracles*

BOOK I: Life's Big Questions, Relationships, Work and Money

Reverend Diane C. Lund

#1 Amazon Bestselling Contributing Author

Interactive Book With Over 15 Introductory Videos

dianelundmiracles.com

To Get Your Life Right Side Up

Turn Your World Upside Down

DEDICATION

This book is dedicated to loving our brothers
and sisters, each and every one.
No exceptions.

"To love another person is to see the face of God."

Les Misérables

CONNECT WITH OUR COMMUNITY

Join Reverend Diane C. Lund and her community of like-minded spiritual students online to further engage with the material presented in this book.

VISIT THE WEBSITE: DIANELUNDMIRACLES

The website is designed to be an online lighthouse and divine classroom that guides, inspires, and awakens your spirit.

- www.dianelundmiracles.com
- www.dianelundmiracles.ca

LIKE OUR FACEBOOK PAGES

- www.facebook.com/dianelundmiracles
- www.facebook.com/groups/dianelundmiracles

FREE ELECTRONIC MONDAY MIRACLE MOMENT CARDS

Receive weekly downloadable cards with a quote from *A Course in Miracles* by email every Monday. Sign up:

- www.bit.ly/mondaymiracles

WATCH MONDAY MIRACLE MOMENT VIDEOS

Join our closed Facebook group to view short videos about each of the Diane Lund Miracle cards.

- www.facebook.com/groups/dianelundmiracles

ORDER DIANE LUND MIRACLE CARD DECKS

The Diane Lund Miracle cards come in eight different coloured decks: Rose, Tangerine, Marigold, Aqua, Jade, Violet, Orchid, and Crimson.
Order online. www.dianelundmiracles.ca/shop

BOOKS IN THE WORKS

Turn Your World Upside Down To Get Your Life Right Side Up! Reverse Thinking Based on *A Course in Miracles*. Book II: Health, Conflict and Fear, and Happiness.

The Language of Love from A to Z.
A quick guide to the meaning of specific words as used in *A Course in Miracles*.
This beautiful e-book is in full colour and is intended to help students get clarity about *A Course in Miracles*.

WARNING: SOME LANGUAGE MAY OFFEND!

If this book frightens you…**good**!

If words like "God," "spirit," and "spirituality" bring up deep resistance…**good**!

If this book makes you angry, frustrated, confused, or annoyed…**good**!

For this could mean you are up against one, some, or all of your internal blocks…**good**!

Why?
Because in the Introduction to *A Course in Miracles*, it says:

> *"The course does not aim at teaching the meaning of love,*
> *for that is beyond what can be taught.*
> *It does aim, however, at removing the blocks*
> *to the awareness of love's presence*
> *which is your natural inheritance."*

T, Introduction: 6-7

In order to have more love in our lives, we first must discover how and why we block love. Any strong negative reactions point to the presence of a possible block. **Good**! That's the place to start.

WELCOME

This book is offered as a chance for you to:
- get curious,
- ask questions,
- explore your thinking, and ultimately
- remove the blocks to the awareness of love's presence in your life.

And why would you want to do that?

So you can live a happier, more peaceful life!

WATCH THE INTRODUCTORY VIDEOS BY SCANNING THE QR CODES
Note: You can download a QR scanner for free off the Internet if you do not already have one on your phone.

At the beginning of each chapter, you will find a short video on the main theme of the chapter. All you have to do is scan the QR code and the video will play.

I hope you enjoy these videos; creating them was a magical experience. I was at a writing retreat in France in the spring of 2018, and when I came upon a beautiful setting during my daily walks, I would hear an inner directive to shoot a video in that spot. I would signal my publisher, who was on the trip with me, and together we would pick a chapter title and start recording. All of the videos felt truly guided and full of spirit, and many were shot in just one take. It was amazing to see them unfold. There were no scripts and no plans. I simply trusted my inner guidance, and I was amazed to see the results. In many ways, creating these videos was a miracle for me, as I hope watching them will be for you.

Before my writing trip to France, I had never even heard of the Dordogne region. I could not have planned these videos in these amazing locations because I literally did not know these places even existed. Spirit is so amazing! Learning to trust and allow spirit to guide you opens the door to so many amazing possibilities in your life.

SEE THE AMAZING DORDOGNE REGION OF FRANCE AND THE *MAISON DE LA LIBELLULE.*

During the retreat, I stayed at a beautiful property in Bayac, France, located in the department of Dordogne in the Aquitaine region. In the introductory videos, you will see the beautiful and charming property and home of Tracey and Andy Antliffe. Their place is called *La Maison de la Libellule* and can be found at www.facebook.com/lamaisondelalibellule/

Both Tracey and Andy were amazing hosts, and their holiday home, or *gîte*, is available for rent. I highly recommend a journey to this part of the world to see *France's 100 Most Beautiful Villages* and to stay at their tranquil property. For me, visiting this region of France was like walking into a real-life fairy tale.

Here's a toast to Tracey and Andy and their gorgeous property!

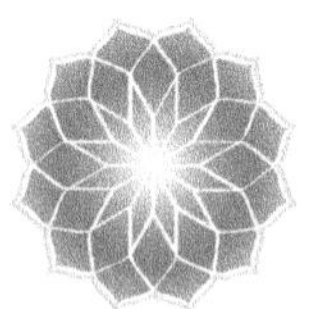

TABLE OF CONTENTS

PART ONE
LIFE'S BIG QUESTIONS:
The Ones My Mom Could Not Answer

PART FOUR
LET'S GET PRACTICAL:
Putting Reverse Thinking Into Action

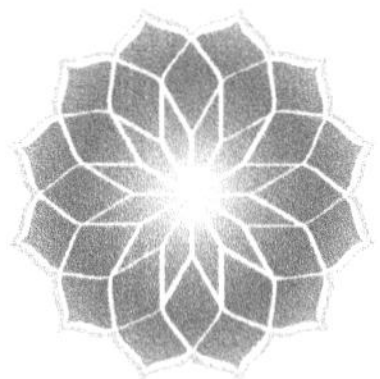

INTRODUCTION
A Course in Miracles

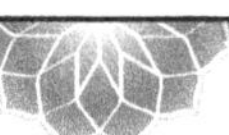

Introduction: What *A Course In Miracles* Means To Me. *A Course in Miracles* is many things to me. The curriculum is to know thyself. Watch this video to learn how *A Course in Miracles* can change your life.

http://bit.ly/IntroBookI

A. MY LOVE AFFAIR WITH *A COURSE IN MIRACLES*

INITIALLY UNIMPRESSED

I have had a torrid love affair with *A Course in Miracles*, and like some famous classic love affairs it all started with indifference. When I first came across this book, I would not give it the time of day. Here's why.

I was introduced to the book in the early 1980s, and the minute I opened it, I was horrified. The pages were paper-thin, like the bible. Plus, the book appeared to really be three books:
- *A Course in Miracles* Text
- A *Workbook for Students* containing 365 lessons, one for each day of the year
- A *Manual for Teachers*

Worst of all for me at the time, the book used a lot of Christian terminology. I did not attend church as a child, and although I had sought out religion in my teenage years, I had left it in my late teens on the advice of my pastor. He said, "The church does not have the answers you are looking for. You need to go on a spiritual search to find the answers to the questions that plague your mind."

I followed his advice and left the church. So, why should I now pick up something loaded with Christian terminology when I believed I had already explored that path?

DRIVEN TO MY KNEES

A Course in Miracles sat on my shelf for years as I ignored it and "ran around" reading every other spiritual book I could get my hands on. After flirting with Buddhism and Taoism and having a full-fledged crush on Eckankar, I thought of myself as a spiritual seeker, looking for love and the deep meaning of life.

Then, as the universe would have it, I got reintroduced to my future spiritual love one night when my current human romantic relationship had driven me to my knees.

Please God, I prayed, *please help me understand why I am in so much pain.*

You see, I had recently discovered my boyfriend had not one but multiple affairs. I learned this at a month-long program devoted to self-awareness at the Haven on Gabriola Island, British Columbia, Canada. He had first admitted this at a private meeting with one of our group leaders, who urged him to come forward in the group and tell me the truth about what was going on in our relationship. This means I learned this truth in front of about sixty other people. To say I was in shock and in deep emotional pain would be an understatement.

Later at home, driven to my knees in pain, I noticed the book *A Course in Miracles* sitting on my shelf. I took the book off the shelf, closed my eyes and repeated my prayer.

Please God, please help me. Then I randomly opened the book and read the following quote.

> *"Unfairness and attack are one mistake,*
> *so firmly joined that where one is perceived the other must be seen.*
> *You cannot be unfairly treated.*
> *The belief you are is but another form of the idea*
> *you are deprived by someone not yourself…*
> *you have no enemy except yourself."*
>
> T, 26, X, 3:1-6

What? My boyfriend had had multiple affairs! Not one, but many. I most certainly felt unfairly treated. I was in disbelief. I was outraged. But, I read on.

> *"Beware of the temptation to perceive yourself unfairly treated.*
> *In this view, you seek to find an innocence that is not theirs but yours alone,*
> *and at the cost of someone else's guilt.*
> *Can innocence be purchased by the giving of your guilt to someone else?"*
>
> T, 26, X, 4:1-3

I sat back. I couldn't believe it. I didn't believe it. But, somewhere within my being, a small and very quiet voice said clearly, *This is the truth!*

I didn't like it. In fact, I hated what the book was saying to me, but something inside knew that my prayer had just been answered. I was reading a truth, even if I didn't understand it. I knew this not in an intellectual way, but rather, in a deep, heartfelt way.

It simply felt right.

Right there and then, I knew I'd better find a way to continue this confounding conversation. More than anything, I wanted to understand why my inner voice had said to me, *This is the truth!*

IT ALL SOUNDS LIKE GREEK TO ME

I sought out and attended my first *A Course in Miracles* reading and study group in the late 1980s. At first, I could not understand what the book was saying. It literally all sounded like Greek to me. But the other students in my study group said, "Most people don't understand a word when they start. Don't worry about understanding the message. Just let the language flow over you. Eventually, the ideas and meaning will start to emerge."

And surprisingly, that's exactly what happened. I think it is like being immersed in another language. At first, nothing makes sense. Then a phrase or two seem to pop out at you. You understand a little, but you are struggling to stay with any conversation. However, you are intrigued. You want to know more, so you hang in. And that is how my real relationship with *A Course in Miracles* began.

I simply hung in there.

(Note: If you want to know how I resolved my dilemma of feeling unfairly treated, look to Part Two: Chapter 7 and read the section entitled FAIRNESS: Am I Unfairly Treated?)

WHATEVER I COULD THROW AT THE BOOK, I DID!

Over the next twenty-five years, I would:

- love the course,
- hate the course,
- put the course back on the shelf,
- take it off the shelf,
- start my own course study group,
- struggle with the ideas,
- reject the ideas,
- understand the ideas,
- throw the book across the room,
- retrieve it,
- highlight it,
- love it,
- ignore it,
- rummage through my bookshelf to find it,
- sit in awe with it,
- curse it,
- feel endless gratitude for it,
- wake up in the middle of the night to read it, and quite frankly,
- everything else you can throw at the book.

Studying *A Course in Miracles* has, in every way, been an internal love affair motivated by painful external events. And that is how I believe most people come to the course: they come beat up by life and often driven to their knees because the world just seems too harsh and too cruel to bear any longer. They are often exhausted from:

- fighting,
- retreating,
- hiding,
- trying,
- striving, and
- working too hard,

until at long last they wave the white flag of surrender in their minds.

This moment of surrender can change everything. When I stopped fighting myself and just did as the course asked – apply the lessons to my everyday world – my life did in fact become easier. My heart cracked open and the light shone within, and with that, the drama in my life started to subside. I got up off my knees, stopped pleading for the world to change, and changed my mind about the world instead.

How did I do that?

I changed my perceptions. I changed my thoughts. And ultimately, the world fell open at my feet and love emerged all around me – like a beautiful love story.

My inner questions were at last being answered. After decades of searching for solutions, I finally decided that *A Course in Miracles* was indeed my life-long spiritual path.

Please note: I do not expect it to be your path.

However, if and when *A Course in Miracles* begins to speak to your soul and you feel as I do, you want to share the love. You want to extend the love. So, now it is my time to share my:

- stories,
- struggles,
- experiences, and
- thoughts

so that perhaps you too can ***Turn Your World Upside Down To Get Your Life Right Side Up!***

B. WHAT *A COURSE IN MIRACLES* MEANS TO ME

A Course in Miracles is many things to me. **The curriculum is to *know thyself*.**
- It can provide a way to find your own internal teacher – the small, still voice within that speaks for God. In the course, this is referred to as the Holy Spirit.
- It can train your mind to think from love in every situation.
- It is about unlearning wrong-minded thinking and moving into right-minded thinking or miracle-minded thinking.
- It is a return to love.
- It is a short and direct path to God or the love that is eternal.
- It is an individual spiritual study guide.

You do not need a study group to explore the course's teachings, but I have certainly found that being in *A Course in Miracles* reading and study groups and eventually leading these groups in my home was extremely helpful.

The concepts, while ultimately simple, usually bring up deep resistance from the ego part of the mind. Most of us have been taught a way to live, to see, and to be that is ultimately 180-degrees from what *A Course in Miracles* teaches. So, we need to change our thinking about what works and what doesn't.

Changing our thinking can be challenging, and having a support group to discuss the work has been comforting and necessary for my own process.

APPLICATION AND EXPERIENCE ARE KEY!

Finally, for me, the course emphasizes application rather than theory and experience rather than theology. You must experience the course concepts for yourself; no one can do this internal work for you. I love how the course puts it in the Introduction to the Workbook For Students:

> *"Remember only this; you need not believe the ideas,*
> *you need not accept them, and you need not even welcome them.*
> *Some of them you may actively resist.*
> *None of this will matter, or decrease their efficacy.*
> *But do not allow yourself to make exceptions in applying the ideas the workbook contains,*
> *and whatever your reactions to the ideas may be, use them.*
> *Nothing more than that is required."*
>
> W, Introduction, 9:1-4

Essentially, the course is not something you just read – it is something you must experience and ultimately prove to yourself. No one else can do it for you.

"I am responsible for what I see."

T, 21, II, 2:3

When you experience that you can change your mind as well as your world, the real excitement begins. You are on the spiritual path to freedom. Personally, I have felt like a spiritual detective – hunting down the clues and following the signs that have led me to find more peace and happiness in my life. Ultimately, I believe it will lead me to my true, authentic self and my spiritual home.

"This course offers a very direct and a very simple learning situation,
and provides the Guide Who tells you what to do.
If you do it, you will see that it works.
Its results are more convincing than its words.
They will convince you that the words are true.
By following the right Guide, you will learn the simplest of all lessons:
By their fruits ye shall know them, and they shall know themselves."

T, 9, V, 9:1-6

This book is really about my personal experience applying the ideas of the course to my own life. It has not always been pretty. The ideas can be downright frightening because, in short, they are asking us to give up the part of ourselves that most of us have spent decades building – our individuality and our specialness. We are very particular about our likes and dislikes, and we hold on to what we think makes us unique from others. The course not only challenges these ideas, it explains how dangerous and painful holding on to these ideas truly is for all of us.

A Course in Miracles is no **child's play**.
- It asks you to search your mind.
- It asks you to question the very fabric of your life and how you live it.

In this way, it appears dangerous, scary, and frightening to our egos.

We are generally comfortable with our life as we know it. So be forewarned: your ego thoughts will fight for survival. Your ego does not want you to uncover the ways it keeps pain and suffering alive. But, if you want to live a more peaceful life, there is no other way but to dive in and look at what is uncomfortable and scary to you. I love this Joseph Campbell quote: *"The cave you fear to enter holds the treasure you seek."*

C. WHAT IS *A COURSE IN MIRACLES?*

Many people may not have heard of *A Course in Miracles*. Or, they have heard the title but they are not sure what it is about. I think the book is well summarized in its own preface. Below is a brief summary of what it says.

SELF-STUDY SPIRITUAL THOUGHT SYSTEM

A Course in Miracles is a complete self-study spiritual thought system and a way in which some people will be able to find their own internal teacher.

It is a three-step curriculum consisting of the:
- *A Course in Miracles* text,
- Workbook for Students, and
- Manual for Teachers.

IT IS BUT ONE VERSION OF THE UNIVERSAL CURRICULUM

A Course in Miracles teaches that the way to universal love and peace – or remembering God – is by undoing guilt through forgiving others. The book focuses on healing relationships and making them holy (whole). It emphasizes that it is but one version of the universal curriculum, of which there are many. Consequently, even though the language of the course is that of traditional Christianity, it expresses a non-sectarian, non-denominational spirituality. *A Course in Miracles* is therefore a universal spiritual teaching, not a religion.

THE TEXT IS THEORETICAL

The text of *A Course in Miracles* presents the theory of the course. It presents two thought systems, the real and the unreal. The real world is under one law: the law of love, or God. There are no changes and no time. Truth is unalterable and eternal. On the other hand, the unreal world is the world of perception, which is based on time and change. It is the world of birth, death, and personal conflict. Conflict arises because we all believe different things. To end the conflict, the course says we must first end the conflict in our minds between the two warring thought systems:
- the thought system of ego, which is based in sin, guilt, and fear, and
- the thought system of the Holy Spirit, which is based in love.

A Course in Miracles asks us to listen within to hear the Voice for God, which is the Holy Spirit.

The Holy Spirit was placed as a communication link between God and his creations when they decided to believe they had separated from him. The Holy Spirit is the Voice for Love. The text explains the basis for fear and guilt and how they can be overcome through miracles – which are defined as maximal expressions of love – and change perceptions (which are changing and personal) into knowledge (which is eternal and non-personal).

THE WORKBOOK IS PRACTICAL

The Workbook for Students consists of 365 lessons – an exercise for each day of the year.

> *"Without the practical application the Workbook provides,*
> *the Text would remain largely a series of abstractions which would hardly suffice*
> *to bring about the thought reversal at which the course aims."*
>
> Preface: ix

This one-year training program begins the process of changing the student's mind and perceptions from fear-based thinking to love-based thinking. This year of lessons is not intended to bring one's learning to completion. As stated in the preface of the course:

> *"At the end, the reader is left in the hands of his or her own Internal Teacher,*
> *Who will direct all subsequent learning as He sees fit."*
>
> Preface: ix-x

THE MANUAL FOR TEACHERS

The Manual for Teachers provides answers to some of the more likely questions a student might ask. It also includes clarification on a number of terms the course uses, explaining them within the theoretical framework of the text and their practical application through the workbook.

WHO WROTE *A COURSE IN MIRACLES?*

A Course in Miracles was scribed by Dr. Helen Schucman, a clinical and research psychologist and tenured associate professor of medical psychology, through a process of inner dictation she identified as coming from Jesus. She was assisted by Dr. William Thetford, her department head and tenured professor of medical psychology at Columbia University's College of Physicians and Surgeons in New York City.

WHEN WAS *A COURSE IN MIRACLES* PUBLISHED?

A Course in Miracles was first published in 1975, the year Dr. Schucman assigned copyright of the course to the Foundation for Inner Peace (FIP). In 1996, FIP assigned the copyright and trademark to the Foundation for *A Course in Miracles* (FACIM).

There are currently millions of copies of the course in circulation worldwide. Translations in Afrikaans, Bulgarian, Chinese, Croatian, Danish, Dutch, Finnish, French, German, Hebrew, Italian, Norwegian, Polish, Portuguese, Romanian, Russian, Slovene, Spanish, and Swedish are also available, with many other translations now in progress.

A COURSE IN MIRACLES SUMMED UP

The introductory section of *A Course in Miracles* text sums up the whole course in the following way:

> *"This is A Course in Miracles.*
> *It is a required course.*
> *Only the time you take it is voluntary.*
> *Free will does not mean that you can establish the curriculum.*
> *It means only that you can elect what you want to take at a given time.*
> *The course does not aim at teaching the meaning of love,*
> *for that is beyond what can be taught.*
> *It does aim, however, at removing the blocks to the awareness of love's presence,*
> *which is your natural inheritance.*
> *The opposite of love is fear, but what is all-encompassing can have no opposite.*
>
> *This Course can therefore be summed up very simply in this way:*
> *Nothing real can be threatened.*
> *Nothing unreal exists.*
> *Herein lies the peace of God."*

T, Introduction, 1-2

MY EXPERIENCE

Something about the above introductory statement always resonates deep within my being. I find it endlessly comforting to read, *"Nothing real can be threatened. Nothing unreal exists."* At first, this statement just felt right to me and encouraged me to pursue the teachings of the course. In addition I liked the idea that the course did not say it was the only way. It says it is *"just one version of the universal curriculum,"* and that also seemed to ring true to me! In my experience, different people and personalities resonate with different paths. In the end, I believe everyone must personally choose their own way, and I honour their choice.

DEEP GRATITUDE

I have deep and profound gratitude for Helen Schucman and Bill Thetford, who brought *A Course in Miracles* to the world, and to Gloria and Kenneth Wapnick, PhD, founders of the Foundation for *A Course in Miracles*. Thank you from the bottom of my heart for your tireless work and enthusiasm for the material. This book covers my journey with *A Course in Miracles* and how the course principles were experienced in my life. My hope is that my stories might open a door or a window in your mind to find and study the course material, as I believe it has the potential to lead anyone back to their authentic self and true origins as eternal love.

D. HOW THIS BOOK IS ORGANIZED.

THE OPENING COUPLET

Western Thinking: this is the dominant thinking of the Western world, which is common but not universal. I say it is *Western thinking* because I believe *Eastern thinking* is often quite different.

Reverse Thinking: this is an opposite way of viewing the world from traditional Western thinking. It is the system of thought that is presented in the book *A Course in Miracles*.

MY PERSONAL EXPERIENCE

What follows the couplet is my personal experience with the reversal in thought, which shows how I came to believe many of them.

SUPPORTING QUOTES FROM *A COURSE IN MIRACLES*

After my personal story is some reflection of the basic principle illustrated within it. This is followed by quotes from *A Course in Miracles* that reference where this principle is discussed in the book. If you feel intrigued, you can look up a quote and go deeper into this topic yourself.

THERE ARE NO RULES – READ WHAT INTERESTS YOU IN ANY ORDER

There is no need to read this book from beginning to end. You can start in the middle, at the end, or at any random page. There is no right way or wrong way, there is just your own **DIVINE INNER GUIDANCE (D.I.G.)** to point you to the sections that will be the most relevant for you.

E. HOW TO FIND QUOTES IN *A COURSE IN MIRACLES* (ACIM)

Published by the Foundation for Inner Peace
Combined Volume (Third Edition) copyrighted 2007 by the Foundation for *A Course in Miracles*
www.facim.org

Quotes from *A Course in Miracles* will be referenced in the following manner:

A COURSE IN MIRACLES TEXT
T: Chapter, Section, Paragraph / Verse: Line

WORKBOOK FOR STUDENTS
W: Lesson Number, Section, Paragraph / Verse: Line

MANUAL FOR TEACHERS
M: Page Number, Section, Paragraph / Verse: Line

EXAMPLE: T, 9, V, 4:1-4
Text (T), Chapter Number (9), Subhead (V), Verse (4): Lines (1-4)

LISTEN!

Listen.
It is in there!
A small, still voice that patiently
sits and waits, for your attention.
Like a song in your heart, it never leaves you.
It waits for you to join it,
to joyously sing it out.
When you least expect it, you hear it ring in your heart,
like a clear crystal bell hanging in the church tower of your soul.

Reverend Diane C. Lund

PART ONE

LIFE'S BIG QUESTIONS:
The Ones My Mom
Could Not Answer

"Reality is merely an illusion, albeit a very persistent one."
Albert Einstein

INTRODUCTION

Right from the time I was young, I started to ask my mom what I call "**THE BIG QUESTIONS.**" You know the type – they go something like:

- Why are we here?
- Is there a God?
- How can we talk to God?
- Where do we go when we die?

These are the questions no one seemed to be able to answer to my satisfaction. But I was stubborn, and so I kept asking them to anyone who would listen.

My mother would try to shut me down. "Diane," she would say, "do not bother our friends with all your questions. Try to keep your mouth shut and be a good girl."

Well, I did try to be a good girl and not ask our friends embarrassing questions. But unfortunately, my enquiring mind wanted to know:

- Where do we come from?
- Where do we go?
- How come there are no real satisfying answers?

In my personal pursuit for answers, I went down many different paths. My parents were not religious and we did not go to church. My dad believed we come from dust and return to dust. He was, in his own words, "a man of science." So, most of my metaphysical musings were dismissed. If I wanted answers, I had to look elsewhere.

SEARCHING FOR A SPIRITUAL HOME

I went to various churches in my teens in search of a spiritual home. I was curious and interviewed many a priest, minister, and pastor with a long list of questions. In the end, I decided to join a church my girlfriend went to because I liked the pastor there. He ran a youth group which seemed to be open to my ongoing inquiries.

WANT TO GO TO HEAVEN?

While I was at that church, I learned that if I wanted to get to heaven, I needed to get baptized. Well, I wanted heaven for my family and myself. Who doesn't? That seemed like a no-brainer. So, I set off to convince everyone at home that we all needed to get baptized. It took a little time, but eventually my devoted parents agreed and we all went to church and got baptized.

I am certain that their submission to my request was more of an effort to get me to shut up than anything else. Regardless, I was relieved. I certainly did not want to go to heaven without my mom and dad.

CONFIRMATION

The next step was to get confirmed in my church – a sacrament aimed to confirm my faith, as it was, and become endowed with God's holy spirit. I needed to study the bible, so I worked at learning the names of all the bible chapters and what was basically said within each one. Then, we were given a test to see what we had learned. I passed with flying colours.

I remember having to dress up all in white (like a bride) and getting presented to the church congregation on Sunday morning. Getting confirmed meant I could now take communion – or rather, take the body and blood of Christ in the form of grape juice and a cracker. It was a big day in my life. I was happy and proud, but I was still far from having my all my questions answered. A few of the lingering questions that kept plaguing me, in my thoughts:

- *What was Jesus' last name?*
- *Why do we need to be baptized to get in to heaven? What if I lived in Africa and was never introduced to the idea of baptism? Would I go to hell just because I was born in a different country? (That thought seemed massively unfair to me.)*
- *Why would a loving God reject or bar people from heaven just because they were born in a different country?*
- *Why would a loving God punish people? (That does not seem like a loving thing to do!)*
- *Why would a loving God accept some people and not all people?*

Finally, with true concern and love, my pastor told me that I should go on a spiritual quest to answer my unending list of questions. He informed me, "Unfortunately, the answers you are looking for do not lie within this church."

Bummer. Of course, I knew that by now, but I wanted what I wanted and what I wanted was easier answers. I wanted someone to tell me what I wanted to know. I didn't want to go searching again. I had to admit, though, that he was confirming what I already knew inside of myself. In the end, I was grateful for his honesty and guidance.

SEARCHING FOR A SPIRITUAL HOME

So, I left the church (and Christianity, or so I thought) in my late teens and started a sincere spiritual search.

- I read about all types of religious or spiritual paths.
- I became interested in Taoism.
- I explored Buddhism and Buddhist principles.
- I stumbled upon ideas I liked and ideas I did not like.
- I did NOT find a spiritual home.

ECKANKAR – THE SCIENCE OF SOUL TRAVEL

I had a profound and haunting dream that led me to discover **Eckankar: The Science of Soul Travel,** as it was known at that time.

But before I tell you that story, I need to fill you in on a little background for you to understand the impact my dream had on me.

THE NUMBER TWENTY-THREE ALWAYS HELD SIGNIFICANCE FOR ME

As a child, I always thought I would discover why I was here when I turned twenty-three years old. Go figure. I did not know why I thought that; I just decided this when I was little and held on to the idea.

Also, although my actual birthday is April 27th, I held a long-harboured desire to have been born on October 23rd. It sounded like the right day to be born to me. So, throughout my teen years I celebrated two birthdays each year: my actual birthday and my preferred birthday. Of course, I celebrated my preferred birthday in my mind and only occasionally mentioned it to my friends. I knew it was just a pretend birthday, but it seemed to hold some type of deep significance for me.

THE QUEEN OF MELANCHOLY

Fast forward to my twenties. In those years, I referred to myself as the "Queen of Melancholy." I had so many questions that remained unanswered. Here are just a few thoughts that possessed my mind:

- Where you were born in the world seemed to have a direct correlation with whether you were more likely to starve to death, be a slave, be born poor, die young, and not get an education (especially if you were a girl).
- People fought and killed each other in senseless wars where they claimed God was their motivation. Well, that seemed like a massive contradiction to me.
- I couldn't believe the hypocrisy, unfairness, cruelty, and injustice I saw on the nightly news.

Thinking about these things drove me to be full of melancholy. I wanted answers, but the more I looked around and listened to the news, the more I felt depressed and longed for a better way.

BACK TO THE DREAM

One night, in my early twenties, I heard a voice in my dream ask me to "go to the mountain."

I was not sure what this inner voice of authority meant so I questioned it. *What mountain are you talking about?*

THE mountain, the voice answered, as if I knew what that meant. I asked again and again, but then I finally stopped arguing, closed my eyes and said in my dream, *Take me to THE mountain.*

When I opened my eyes, I was at the bottom of a huge mountain. I started to climb up the mountainside to a building high up in the clouds. Somehow I knew the building was a monastery where people of ancient wisdom lived.

On the way to the monastery, I passed many people who were also trying to get to the top. Eventually, I reached the building and crawled in through a small, open window. When I stood on the floor and looked around, I saw the room held only a bed and a few spiritual-looking objects.

I walked out into the hall and found monks in robes moving towards a central room, so I followed them. I learned they were called Breatharians. They did not eat food. Instead, they sustained themselves by living off of the *prana* – that is, the essence of God energy that surrounds everyone – in the air. I was fascinated. No eating, just breathing. Interesting.

I went back to my room and looked out the window and down the mountain slope. What I saw were people hurt and bleeding trying to climb up the mountain. I was deeply concerned for these people, and I wanted to help them.

I ran back into the hall and asked the monks to help me, but they laughed and continued on their way. I was very annoyed. Why was everyone ignoring the plight of these poor people?

I went back to the window, determined to help them myself. Miraculously, I was now able to stretch my arms and upper body down the mountain slope. I lifted the people up to the top of the mountain and put them outside the building where I was staying. Just like me, they then crawled inside the building through open windows. As they did this, all their wounds, bruises, and cuts were healed. Instantly, I seemed to understand why the wounded victims crawling up the mountainside did not upset the monks. They somehow knew nothing was truly hurting these people, and that all would be fine once they reached their destination. I found the idea fascinating.

A SPIRITUAL INITIATION

Still within my dream, I went to sleep in the room with the small bed. Upon awakening, I was told to follow a monk as it was time for my initiation.

Initiation into what? I asked, but no one answered my question. So, I followed. I was taken to a balcony and asked to look at the amazing mountain across from me. It was breathtaking in size, and as the sun rose and hit its slopes, the mountain was bathed in a golden-pink light of radiant glory.

I was asked to close my eyes, and suddenly it seemed as if a part of me rose up out of my body and soared to the very height of the glowing gold mountain. When I reached the top, I seemed to be hurled down the entire mountainside to its base. Just as I was going to hit the ground, I started to spin upwards to the top of the mountain again. This flying up and down the mountainside continued many times until I lost all sense of where I was or what was happening. Finally, it ended and I awoke in my bed in the monastery, only to then awaken again in my real physical home.

What a dream! The images of flying up and down the golden mountainside possessed me for days. I just could not shake the feelings and the clear mental images.

A FEW DAYS LATER…
I happened to be in a library when a book fell from a shelf while I was walking by. On the cover of the book was the mountain from my dream. I was shocked. It surely was no coincidence that this book literally landed right at my feet, so I knew I had to read it.

The book was about Eckankar: The Science of Soul Travel. In the book, I read that Eckankar's spiritual year ends at midnight on October 22nd, which means that October 23rd is Eckankar's New Year's Day. Well, that explained the significance of my lifelong obsession with October 23rd – apparently, I had been celebrating Eckankar's spiritual new year since my youth. Instantly, I felt this spiritual path was my fate.

For ten years, I followed the path of Eckankar because I felt I had been led to it, not by the outer world but by my own inner world. During this time, I learned so many amazing things about spirituality, soul travel, meditation, levels of spiritual awareness, and several other fascinating topics. For a decade, I thought I had found my spiritual home.

However, everything on this physical earth plane shifts and changes. After years of study, I found the Eckankar organization was full of inner turmoil. I was not interested in all the politics of the organization, and I felt I needed to leave. I did not think what I had learned was not true, I just felt let down by human beings who always seem to fight amongst themselves. Surely there must be another path that would not be in conflict with itself.

THE SEARCH CONTINUES
- I left Eckankar.
- I left relationships.
- I left jobs.
- I left residences.

I left it all in search of something better, something more fulfilling. It was like stepping from stone to stone. Once, I had a beautiful dream about this spiritual-seeking process.

STEPPING STONES TO TRUTH

In this dream, I was standing at the edge of a lake that I wanted to cross. I closed my eyes and asked God for assistance, and when I opened my eyes a rock rose out of the water. I took a step and stood upon it. Then, another rock appeared in the lake just beyond the one I was standing on. When I stepped on this new rock, the one behind me disappeared back into the water. As I continued to step forward a new rock would appear, and as my foot left a rock it would disappear back into the depths of the lake. In my dream, I crossed the lake as if I had walked on water.

Suddenly, an invisible voice said to me, *All is given at the appointed time. You need to have faith that what is needed will always appear. There is truly nothing to fear. Simply ask and you shall receive.*

What a simple but truly profound message and demonstration of the power of faith. I awoke from my dream and knew I did not need to worry about my next step – all would be shown to me in the right time.

A SMORGASBORD OF SPIRITUAL DELIGHTS

I continued along the smorgasbord of spiritual delights for many years. I read almost every book on spiritual growth and self-help I could get my hands on, and I travelled and explored many different paths. Along the way, I was given *A Course in Miracles*, but it did not immediately appear to me as the way, the truth, and the light. It was full of Christian terminology, and I believed Christianity had not provided me with the answers I needed. In fact, my pastor had specifically told me I would not find the answers there. So, I initially felt a great deal of resistance to the course language and material. In fact, it took me over twenty years of studying *A Course in Miracles* before I finally knew it would be my path for the rest of my life.

Today, I am committed to *A Course in Miracles*, and I feel my spiritual seeking has come to an end. I can finally answer the questions that have plagued me for decades, and I feel compelled to help individuals who, like myself, just cannot stop asking those bigger questions.

In reading this book, please know I don't expect you to believe everything I say, or that *A Course in Miracles* says. Everyone searches their own heart and has their own path. Even the course says that it is just one of many paths to the truth. But, as I have found answers here, I knew I needed to share them.

So, here it goes: five of Life's Big Questions answered from a new perspective – a 180-degree perspective I like to call reverse thinking.

# Chapter 1

MIRACLES: Do Miracles Exist?

Western Thinking
- Miracles are rare and difficult.

Reverse Thinking
- Miracles occur naturally.

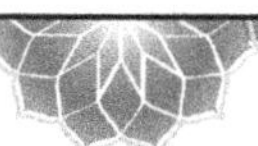

Chapter 1 - Miracles: Do Miracles Exist?
Contrary to public opinion, *A Course in Miracles* says miracles occur naturally and define them as "a shift in perception" from thinking with fear to thinking with love. Watch this video to learn how reverse thinking can put the power of miracles in your hands.

http://bit.ly/1Miracles

MIRACLES OCCUR NATURALLY:
MY PERSONAL EXPERIENCE WITH THIS REVERSE THOUGHT

The Western world's understanding of a miracle is that it is something rare and difficult to achieve. *A Course in Miracles* has an entirely different definition for this word: that it is simply a correction at the level of thought. You may hear *A Course in Miracles* students say, "A miracle is a correction in perception from thinking with fear to thinking with love." Or, they may say a miracle occurs when you go from thinking with your ego or wrong mind (ego-driven thinking based in fear) to thinking with your right mind (spirit-driven thinking based in love). From this perspective, miracles occur naturally. Here's a story from my life that I believe illustrates this course principle.

THE BLUE BUTTERFLY

A few years back, I was wondering if I should write about my experiences with *A Course in Miracles*. I own an advertising company called Creative Wonders Communications, and I have been writing and producing for over three decades. I make my living as a writer, creating radio, print, TV, online ads, outdoor ads, websites – whatever my clients want and need in order for them to grow and expand their local, regional, or national businesses. Generally, though, I do not write about my thoughts and beliefs, other than in my journals. To put my innermost thoughts out in the world felt risky to me; I was full of fear about doing it. If I was to use language from *A Course in Miracles*, I was thinking with my fear-based ego or wrong mind. I was worried about what others might think of me and whether or not I would be harshly judged. So, I asked the Holy Spirit (which *A Course in Miracles* says is the communication link to God), *Do you want me to start writing about A Course in Miracles? If so, please show me a blue butterfly.*

At the time, I believed that was a challenging request! As far as I knew, blue butterflies live primarily in Mexico and South America, and I had never seen one where I live in Vancouver. So, I thought I was asking for something rare and difficult to manifest.

Well, a couple of days later, I went outside in the sunshine to watch all the honey bees working on the hundreds of blossoms clinging to a climbing hydrangea. It was quite a sight. The vine grew right up the side of my house, and it was literally buzzing with activity. As I stood there watching in amazement, suddenly a very tiny blue butterfly flew right across my vision. My mind raced with thoughts.

- *What?*
- *Did I really see that?*
- *A tiny blue butterfly?*
- *Impossible!*

As if in answer to my question, the butterfly flew back across my field of vision.

I could not believe my eyes! I went inside not quite believing what I had seen – perhaps I had been mistaken. I also wondered if my sighting truly counted as it was not the BIG blue butterfly I had imagined.

The next day, I was getting out of my car and heading in my home's front door when I heard my D.I.G. (Divine Inner Guidance) or Holy Spirit say, *Look up and to the left.*

I did, and immediately I started to laugh. There in the corner of my house above the door was a blue metal butterfly that had once been part of a garden ornament. I had stuck it there years ago and had totally forgotten about it. I guess I passed it daily, but since it was above my head and above my sight line, I had not remembered its existence.

Then, it hit me: *I did not say the blue butterfly had to be alive!* I laughed all the way up the stairs. Well, that settled it!

When I was out the next day and heading into a meeting room, I came face to face with a bulletin board where a child had painted a picture of (you guessed it!) a large blue butterfly. There was my message again, sitting there in plain view.

I could feel spirit playing with me. *You thought this would be difficult for us – just wait.*

I continued to run into countless images of blue butterflies over the next few days, but the whole event ended when my friend asked me to go to a meeting at a church where Eben Alexander was going to give a talk about his near-death experience (or NDE, as they are sometimes called).

I didn't really want to go as I had heard many stories of near-death experiences as well as having one myself, so I was already a believer. There was nothing he could say or not say that would ever change my mind. But my friend had a free ticket and really wanted to go, so I agreed to go with her.

When we got to the church, there was a line up down the block as the doors were not yet open. What I noticed right away started to make me laugh, again. Eben's book, entitled **Proof of Heaven,** has a blue butterfly on the front cover and people all around me were clutching his book in their hands. Then, when the doors were opened and we went in the church hall, there was an entire room full of people carrying this book with a blue butterfly on the cover. It was quite a sight. Later, Eben gave his talk, and to thank him for coming and sharing his story, the church representatives gave him (what else?) a framed blue butterfly as a gift. I laughed to myself all the way home.

The universe had certainly answered my question and even played with my fear-based thinking. I thought I had asked the Holy Spirit for something that was hard and difficult, but it was now clear to me that the universe was demonstrating one of the first principles given in *A Course in Miracles:*

> *"There is no order of difficulty in miracles.*
> *One is not harder or bigger than another.*
> *They are all the same."*
>
> T, 1, I, 1-3

I realized that I was the one who thought miracles are hard and difficult. The universe was obviously showing me that the exact opposite is true in a playful and joyful way. This is one experience that helped to change my mind and my perception.

Now I believe there is nothing that the universe, the Creator, the Source cannot arrange or do. It can literally move mountains, as the old biblical saying goes.

Today, I believe that when I keep my thinking and my mind aligned with love and the Holy Spirit, the universe is going to be there for me every step of the way. I felt loved and supported, and I knew I was being told: *Start writing your stories now!*

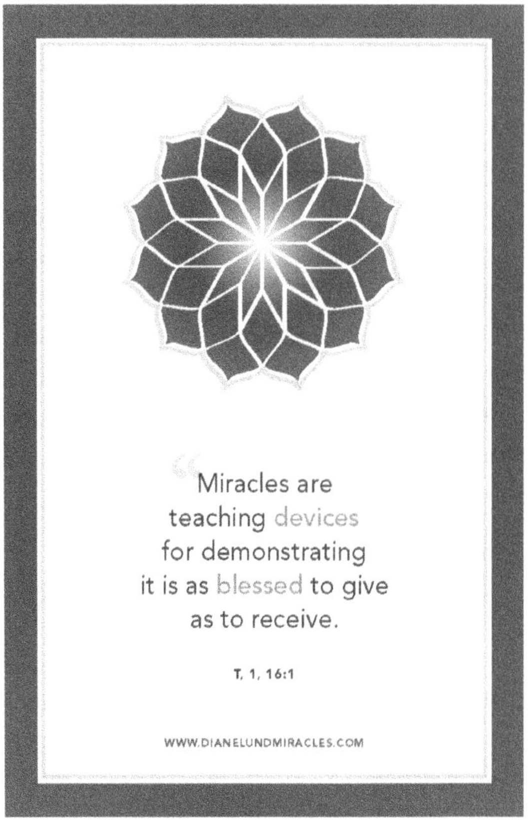

WHAT DOES *A COURSE IN MIRACLES* SAY ABOUT MIRACLES?

The book *A Course in Miracles* is a how-to guide for creating miracles in your own life. Miracles, according to the course, are maximal expressions of love that correct our perception from thinking with fear to thinking with love. It is important to note that, perception and knowledge are different things.

Knowledge is something that is eternal. It does not change from person to person. Knowledge is true for everyone, all the time.

Perception is our individual interpretation of what we see. For example, each of us could watch the same movie and have entirely different stories to tell about what we saw. Some people might say it was so sad, while others might not think it was sad at all. Perception is individual, and it is based in duality. We compare one thing to another thing and come up with our individual opinions. When our opinions do not match, we often get into conflict – this is true out in the world but also within our own minds. You could say we are both outwardly and inwardly conflicted, or at war, with ourselves. All conflict can be attributed to fearful thinking at its root.

- Fear that someone will beat us or punish us.
- Fear that we will be proved wrong.
- Fear that we will run out of money.
- Fear that we will die if we do something out of our comfort zone.

The miracle corrects these fearful perceptions, bringing our mind and thoughts back into alignment with the true, eternal knowledge that always comes from love.

A Course in Miracles starts out by giving fifty different principles that define what a miracle is. I can honestly say that when I read these principles when I first began studying the course, they did not make sense to me. Many of the principles are in opposition to what I was taught in my life. For example, as stated earlier in this chapter, I was taught miracles are rare. However, in *A Course in Miracles*, principle number six provides a different reality:

"Miracles are natural. When they do not occur something has gone wrong."

T, 1, I, 6:1-2

Here are some other definitions of what a miracle is from *A Course in Miracles.*

A MIRACLE IS A CORRECTION

"A miracle is a correction. It does not create, nor really change at all. It merely looks on devastation, and reminds the mind that what it sees is false. It undoes error, but does not attempt to go beyond perception, nor exceed the function of forgiveness."

W, L340, 13. What Is A Miracle? 1:1-4

A MIRACLE CONTAINS THE GIFT OF GRACE

"A miracle contains the gift of grace, for it is given and received as one."

W, L340, 13. What Is A Miracle? 2:1

A MIRACLE INVERTS PERCEPTION

"A miracle inverts perception which was upside down before, and thus it ends the strange distortions that were manifest."

W, L340, 13. What Is A Miracle? 2:3

MIRACLES ARE THE EXPRESSION OF ATONEMENT

"The miracle, or the expression of Atonement, is always a sign of respect from the worthy to the worthy. The recognition of this worth is re-established by the Atonement."

T, 2, VI, 8:1

MIRACLES ARE THE END OF ILLUSION

"Every miracle is but the end of an illusion."

T, 19, IV, A, 6:8

MIRACLES ENTAIL A SUDDEN SHIFT FROM A HORIZONTAL TO VERTICAL PERCEPTION

"The miracles entail a sudden shift from horizontal to vertical perception. This introduces an interval from which the giver and receiver both emerge farther along in time than they would have otherwise been. The miracle thus has the unique property of abolishing time to the extent that it renders the interval of time it spans unnecessary."

T, 1, II, 6:3-5

MIRACLES PLACE THE MIND IN A STATE OF GRACE

"As an expression of what you truly are, the miracle places the mind in a state of grace. The mind then naturally welcomes the Host within and the stranger without."

T, I, III, 7:4-5

MIRACLES ARE EXPRESSIONS OF LOVE

"Miracles occur naturally as expressions of love. The real miracle is the love that inspires them. In this sense everything that comes from love is a miracle."

T, 1, I, 3:1-3

MIRACLES ARE INSTANTS OF RELEASE

"Miracles are the instants of release you offer, and will receive. They attest to your willingness to be released, and to offer time to the Holy Spirit for His use of it."

T, 15, I, 12:4-5

MIRACLES ARE EVERYONE'S RIGHT

"Miracles are everyone's right, but purification is necessary first."

T, 1, I, 7:1-2

MIRACLES ARE THOUGHTS

"Miracles are thoughts. Thoughts can represent the lower or bodily level of experience, or the higher or spiritual level of experience. One makes the physical and the other creates the spiritual."

T, 1, I, 12:1-3

YOU ARE A MIRACLE

"You are a miracle, capable of creating in the likeness of your Creator. Everything else is your own nightmare and does not exist. Only the creations of light are real."

T, 1, I, 24:2-4

 # Chapter 2

JUDGMENT:
DOES GOD JUDGE US?

Western Thinking
- God is the ultimate judge.

Reverse Thinking
- God does not judge.

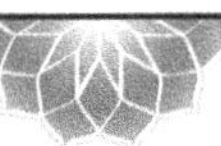

Chapter 2 - Judgment: Does God Judge Us?
A Course in Miracles is all about learning to drop your judgment about other people. The course teaches us that judgment is purely in the human realm and not of God. Watch this video to learn more about the meaning behind this reverse logic.

http://bit.ly/2Judgment

GOD DOES NOT JUDGE:
MY PERSONAL EXPERIENCE WITH THIS REVERSE THOUGHT

Here is a topic with a lot of room for confusion, starting with a simple definition: what is a judgment? I struggled with this idea for a long time. It seemed to me that you need judgment just to move through the world.

For example: I want to cross the road and a car is in the distance.
I judge whether or not I have time to cross the street safely.

However, this is not the type of judgment the course is talking about. Let's call this type of action a simple decision. Every day in this physical world, we need to make lots of decisions. Without making decisions, we would simply sit in our rooms and not go anywhere.

HOW ARE DECISIONS DIFFERENT FROM JUDGMENT?

To figure out the answer to this question, I suggest you start with your feelings. When it is a simple decision, there are no strong feelings. In contrast, when there is a judgment, there is an underlying feeling of discomfort and often a feeling of rejection or dejection. On some level, I am judging what is occurring – I am saying something is not right, or not safe, or not good enough. In this case, I am emphasizing the negative and not the positive. Another way of saying it might be that I am coming from fear and not from love. The bottom line is that judging people and things can feel uncomfortable and can feel like a burden you are physically carrying around on your body – it is like a dead weight that can literally cripple your progress.

I believe we judge situations because we think we know what is best for others and for ourselves, but the truth is that many things remain unseen, unheard, and unfelt in our everyday lives. We are often seeing and hearing with physical eyes and ears rather than spiritual sight and inner listening. We think we know, and so we judge, and often this judgement keeps us from seeing the real truth about people.

Here's a story of how judgment kept me from a loving relationship with my mother.

MY MOM AND THE RED, RED ROSE

My mom came over for Sunday night dinner for as long as she was able to make it up our stairs. She typically arrived around four in the afternoon for a wonderful coconut mango drink and a family catch-up chat. Then we would have a good dinner, and if it was still light out afterwards, she would drive herself back home. During wintertime, when it would get dark early, she would often stay overnight and drive herself home in the morning instead.

One Monday morning, as I made my mom coffee and breakfast, I decided to ask her, "Why has our relationship always felt strained? We fought a lot when I was a teenager, and I'm wondering why we still continue to fight to this day."

My mom seemed to thoughtfully consider this question. She said, "I don't know exactly why that is…but I will think about it and tell you next Sunday."

I thought that was amazing. Usually if I asked a question like that, I was sure to be met with tears and words like, "You are a mean daughter. I don't remember anything like that!"

Next Sunday, my mom came for dinner, and while we were having a drink I asked her if she had thought about my question. She put down her drink carefully and said to me, "Yes, I have thought about it, and what came to me was this: you just did not need me. Right from the time you were a baby, I would hold you and know you did not need me. Your sisters needed me, but not you!"

"Mom," I cried, "That is crazy. Of course I needed you. I was a baby! I needed you to feed me, change me, rock me, dress me, talk to me, and love me."

"No," she said strongly, "you did not need me."

Wow, I thought. Did she really believe that as a baby, I did not need her? I absolutely needed her to survive! I wondered why she would make such a harsh judgment that would set the stage for years of struggles down the road.

Her judgment clearly was that I did NOT need her. Funny, as a child I had perceived just the opposite: SHE did not need ME, except to do her household tasks and chores. Like most children, I had a long list of parental grievances or judgments. I started to voice my thoughts to my mother when suddenly, a miracle occurred!

I heard my D.I.G. (Divine Inner Guidance) asking, *Why are you still knocking on a door that will never open?* The question stopped me in my tracks. Why was I still talking about and trying to fix the pain in my childhood?

An answer came to me in a flash, and I said it out loud: "I do not need to change my mother or change my relationship with my mother. What I need to do is change my thinking about my mother."

Suddenly, there was nothing to **DO** on the outside and everything to **UNDO** in my thinking. As long as I judged my mother for things in my past, I would bring my feelings into my present and project them into my future, causing a never-ending cycle of hurt and harm for both of us. So, I made a bold decision: **to change for good.**

Don't you just love the expression, a *"change for good"*? Following the terminology of the course, I decided to stop aligning with my wrong mind – my ego mind, where I was fearful and hurt – and start aligning with my right mind, where I could come from love.

I wondered, *What can I do to express this change in thinking to my mother?*

In a rash and bold way, I decided I was not going to fight with my mother ever again – instead, I was going to focus on loving her. So, I decided to look for a way to express my new commitment.

Since a red rose is a symbol of love, I decided to get my mother a red rose bush to plant in her yard. On Mother's Day, I gave her the rose with this promise in a card:

> *Mom, this red rose expresses the love I truly feel for you.*
> *I want you to know that this rose is a symbol of my commitment*
> *to never fight with you again.*
> *I only want to give you love, light, and laughter.*
> *Plant this rose in your garden,*
> *and with each new bloom*
> *know my love grows and blossoms for you!*
>
> *Your life-long, loving daughter, Diane*

I have held to this commitment ever since. I decided not to judge my mother or fight with her, and I have kept my word. This decision to drop judgment has changed my relationship with her.

Today, I look for ways to offer her love. And guess what? She often offers her love right back. All that talking, crying, fighting, avoiding, and cursing just created walls, distance, regret, and sadness.

When I decided to let it all go, the miracle occurred.

Do not get me wrong, it is not perfect every day. I do sometimes find myself on a slippery piece of ground where I could easily fall into my old ways of thinking and judging. *Poor me. My mom does not get along with me or love me.* But, I soon remember, *Diane, do you want to continue to suffer around your mother?*

When I drop my judgment and see only love, that is truly what happens – I see only love. And that's a miracle!

Love you Mom!

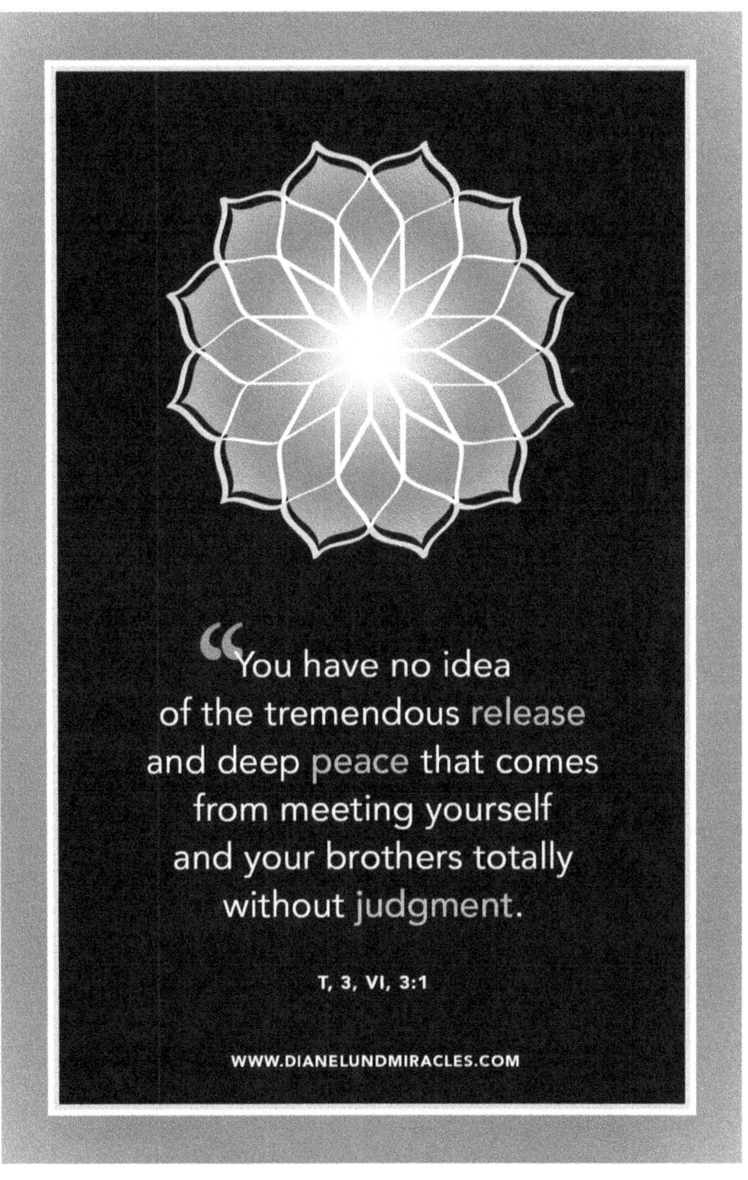

WHAT DOES *A COURSE IN MIRACLES* SAY ABOUT JUDGMENT?

A Course in Miracles is about releasing all the judgments we have that keep us stuck and fearful. When we cannot feel a loving thought, it is because we have a judgment that we may or may not be consciously aware of making and accepting.

The course asks us to look at our judgments and see how they are keeping us from feeling peaceful. Whenever we feel angry, hurt, depressed, or frustrated, we have judgments behind our emotions that are not working in our favour.

In order to free our mind and find peace, we need to seek out our internal judgments and learn to change our mind about what we judge. Ultimately, God never judges because God is pure, unfaltering, and eternal. However, in our duality, we move back and forth between right-minded thinking and left-minded thinking. We are the ones who judge, and if we want to find inner peace, we need to change our minds or our thoughts about our world and the people in it.

Here are some quotes from *A Course in Miracles* that address and expand upon this reverse thinking.

JUDGMENT ALWAYS RESTS ON THE PAST
"Judgment always rests on the past, for past experience is the basis on which you judge. Judgment becomes impossible without the past, for without it you do not understand anything. You would make no attempt to judge, because it would be quite apparent to you that you do not understand what anything means."
T, 15, V, 1:3-5

THE CHOICE TO JUDGE IS THE CAUSE OF THE LOSS OF PEACE
"The choice to judge rather than to know is the cause of the loss of peace."
T, 3, VI, 2:1

JUDGMENT IS THE SETTING OF A PRICE
"There is a price you will pay for judgment, because judgment is the setting of a price. And as you set it you will pay it."
T, 9, II, 9:5-6

JUDGMENT ALWAYS INVOLVES REJECTION

"Judgment always involves rejection. It never emphasizes only the positive aspects of what is judged, whether in you or in others."

T, 3, VI, 2:4-5

THE STRAIN OF CONSTANT JUDGMENT

"The strain of constant judgment is virtually intolerable."

T, 3, VI, 5:6

DEEP PEACE COMES FROM MEETING YOURSELF AND OTHERS WITHOUT JUDGMENT

"You have no idea of the tremendous release and deep peace that comes from meeting yourself and your brothers totally without judgment."

T, 3, VI, 3:1:1

GIVING UP JUDGMENT IS THE PREREQUISITE FOR HEARING GOD'S VOICE

"The giving up of judgment, the obvious prerequisite for hearing God's voice, is usually a fairly slow process, not because it is difficult, but because it is apt to be perceived as personally insulting. The world's training is directed toward achieving a goal in direct opposition to that of our curriculum. The world trains for reliance on one's judgment as the criterion for maturity and strength. Our curriculum trains for the relinquishment of judgment as the necessary condition of salvation."

M, 26, 9, 2:4-7

THIS IS GOD'S FINAL JUDGMENT

"This is God's Final Judgment: 'You are still My Holy Son, forever innocent, forever loving and forever loved, as limitless as your Creator, and completely changeless and forever pure. Therefore, awaken and return to Me. I am your Father and you are My Son.'"

W, L10, What Is The Last Judgment? 5:1-3

# Chapter 3

DEATH: Do We Die?

Western Thinking
- We all die.

Reverse Thinking
- We are all eternal.

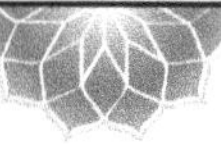

Chapter 3 - Death: Do We Die?
I had a near-death experience (NDE) in my twenties and it radically altered my thoughts on death. Watch this video to learn about the life-transforming wisdom I gained from my NDE.

http://bit.ly/3Death

WE ARE ALL ETERNAL:
MY PERSONAL EXPERIENCE WITH THIS REVERSE THOUGHT

When I was in my early twenties, I was having a rough time coping with my family. My mom had had a nervous breakdown, and I was there to witness her heartbreak and the shattering of her world. My dad was drinking heavily, and I really did not know how to mend my broken family. I was now living away from home and going to university, but I still felt like I was responsible and needed to do something to get my family stitched back together again.

I didn't have the answers, and I knew it.

So, I went to a university counsellor to try and deal with my feelings and my desire to help the ones I loved. I felt sure my dad would drink himself to death and believed my mother would never recover from her inability to cope with my dad's disease and addiction. My father's drinking had gone on for many years, and I was sick of the whole situation – literally.

For a full year, I went to a doctor and complained that there was something wrong with me. I was experiencing pains, and at night I often dreamed I was having labour pains. When I explained what I felt in my body, my doctor told me, "It's all in your mind."

In one way, he was right. In another way, he was dead wrong.

I woke up early one morning in such severe pain that I had to crawl to the phone. I called my mom, who had previously worked as a nurse, and asked her to come to my place and drive me to the hospital as I felt unable to do it myself. She was wonderful; she came right over and did just that. We got to the emergency ward at about five in the morning. My regular doctor was obviously not there at such an early hour, but the hospital staff called him to come in. While I waited for my doctor, an intern in the emergency room met with me. Without giving me a physical exam, he told me I had venereal disease (VD) and to go home. I was shocked by his diagnosis. I knew in my heart (and my body) that this was totally untrue, but I didn't know how to argue with the doctor as I was young and inexperienced with medical things. So, I went out to the waiting room and told my mother what the intern had told me. She was outraged. She asked me if he had given me an internal exam. I told her no.

She continued, "No doctor can just look at you and say you have VD – they need to do tests. He is just making an ignorant decision because you are a young woman."

I knew she was right, but I was in too much pain to comment. My mom and I went back to my apartment, and I told her not to leave me because I knew something terrible was going to happen. She stayed with me for hours while I lay on the couch and waited for the awful event.

Sure enough, three hours later I felt like my body was suddenly being smashed between two very large pieces of lumber. I was covered with sweat in an instant, and just before I passed out, I called out: "Mom, I'm dying."

Mom ran over to me, sat me up, and said, "You are not dying."

Looking into her eyes, I thought, *The only thing I care about is the people I love.* And then I lost consciousness.

When I awoke, I was in a hospital bed with a needle in my arm. They were giving me medicine to treat the diagnosis given by the intern.

I laid in that bed for days, growing weaker and weaker as time passed. They gave me blood transfusions, but eventually all my veins collapsed. I remember the nurses cried when they could not find a vein to put the needle into. Eventually I was too weak to speak, and I thought to myself, *Now I truly am going to die.* At this point, I had been in the hospital for a couple of weeks and was not getting better. The doctors were puzzled.

Finally, they brought in a specialist who examined me, sat me up, and then announced to me, "You are a very sick girl. You should be screaming for help."

Scream, I thought, *I am too weak to even speak.* Then I thought, *Of course I am sick! That is obvious! Tell me something I don't know.*

The good news is that this specialist did tell me something I did not know. He said he believed he knew what was the matter with me and, based on his diagnosis, I was prepped for surgery the next day.

Lying on the operating table, they put me under and the surgery began. They discovered I had a ruptured ovarian cyst, and for weeks my blood had been circulating in my system and clotting around the rupture. I had, in fact, been bleeding internally this whole time. It wasn't good.

I decided I would like to get a better picture of what was going on, so my spirit left my physical body, sat on the ceiling, and watched the operation from above.

As the doctor operated on my physical body, my spirit thought, *Who is the person lying on the stretcher? Certainly, it is not me – I am here on the ceiling.*

I looked down at the body and thought, *I have no idea who that is – it's not me. I am here. I am not even sure if I know the person on the stretcher.*

I felt no attachment to the body undergoing the operation, so I thought, *I might as well leave. The person on the stretcher isn't me, so why stick around? Let's go!* And with that, I made up my mind to leave this sick situation.

I did not know exactly where I was going, but I knew I was going. I turned and headed into the light.

You might wonder how I knew how to do this, and the truth is that I don't know the answer to this question. All I know is that I turned and travelled through the light and finally emerged into a sea of sound and golden-pink light that was ebbing and flowing. I merged with this ocean of light and sound and felt an immediate expansion of complete and utter bliss.

I cried out, *I'm home! I'm home!* over and over again as I felt a multitude of other souls connected to me. It was like being a drop of water in an undulating ocean. I knew who I was, but I was joined with everything and everyone else. The joy I felt was like nothing I have ever experienced on earth. I was just so happy to be home. I wanted to stay there forever, but then an unknown voice called my name. I went to this voice, just like I went into the ocean of light. I don't know how I did this – I somehow seemed to know where to go and what to do, even though the world around me was formless and there was nothing physically moving.

The voice continued, *It's not your time. You have to go back.*

No, I argued, insistent and clear. *I made the decision to leave. I am not going back!*

You have no choice, the voice said gently. And with that, I felt I was being sucked backwards through the tunnel of light and into my physical body in the operating room.

I awoke in the recovery room, furious. I did not want to be there. I wanted to go home – my real home, NOT my earthly home. I was angry that I had returned. The bliss on the other side had been too perfect, and now that I had tasted it. I wanted more.

I did not give up my position easily. It took me a good month to settle down and accept that I had come back to my physical body for a reason. I remembered that the gentle voice had said, *It's not your time.* So, I reasoned there must be more to do here on earth.

From that day forward, my life would never be the same.

The doctors may have saved my physical life with the operation, but I wasn't as thankful for that as much as I was thankful for the depth of understanding that had come back with me from the other side. For the first time, I knew accomplishing things was not so important. Instead, I knew without a doubt the following principles:

- We are not our bodies, we are spirit.
- The body dies, but the spirit never dies.
- The spirit has eternal life.

My experience of looking down on my body during the operation and not knowing who it was, along with the fact that I really had no feeling for it, helped me come to these conclusions.

My near-death experience (NDE) taught me that my true, authentic self was something apart from my physical body and personality. I came back with knowledge about my true, authentic self – that I am:

- something whole and deeply connected to others,
- something blissfully happy, and
- something that has intelligence beyond the physical.

I now knew for certain that the personality and the body called Diane is just here for a short time, and that both the body and the time I appear to live here on earth are illusions. I had proven this truth to myself beyond a shadow of a doubt.

You cannot take this kind of experience away from a person. Once you know, you know. There are no questions, just certainty, and it does not matter whether other people believe you or not. This is an experience of true knowledge and not just individual perception.

Blissfully, I came back with the knowledge that I didn't have to get it all done in just one short lifetime. My near-death experience showed me that I am an eternal spirit, and I came back here to the physical world to share the knowledge of who I truly am when the time was right. And what I have learned since then is that the time is always right.

Ultimately, death is no longer about dying for me. Instead death is about releasing a physical body and returning to my authentic self – my eternal spirit that is connected to everything.

WHAT DOES *A COURSE IN MIRACLES* SAY ABOUT DEATH?

My near-death experience showed me there is no such thing as death. There is only one life – life in a body, and life without a body – and it is the ultimate gift from God or from our Source.

So, why does death appear real to us on this physical plane? We have all known people who have died, and they have not risen from their graves. As a result, our physical eyes tell us they are no longer with us. Perhaps we have to use a different kind of perception to know and understand different things. Perhaps our eyes do not see all that is. Perhaps we need to open our minds and our inner senses to worlds beyond the physical. I know that is what my near-death experience did for me – it confirmed there is more to our existence than what meets our eyes. We are more than our bodies. We are more than just physical.

A Course in Miracles asks us to believe in life eternal and not death eternal. It tells us that death was created by the ego or by fearful thoughts when we decided to separate from our Source. In essence, it says we created the idea of death, then projected it out of our minds and created a physical universe where we could hide from our fear and guilt.

A Course in Miracles also says our thoughts create and manifest what we see and what we experience. This idea is backed up by science. Subatomic, or quantum mechanics, says we are all connected on the subatomic level, where everything is vibrating energy. Our thoughts, which are also vibrating energy, go out from us and interact with the energy web of all reality. When you repeatedly think thoughts over and over, these thought waves attract or magnetize particles in the quantum field that in turn become matter. You literally attract the images to you that match your thinking, both conscious and subconscious. Consequently, if you want to change what you experience, you need to change your mind or your thinking.

Here are some quotes from *A Course in Miracles* that expand upon the idea that we do not die, we are eternal.

DEATH IS THE RESULT OF THE THOUGHT WE CALL THE EGO

"When you accepted the Holy Spirit's purpose in place of the ego's you renounced death, exchanging it for life. We know that an idea leaves not its source. And death is the result of the thought we call the ego, as surely as life is the result of the Thought of God."

T, 19, C, 2:13-14

NO ONE CAN DIE UNLESS HE CHOOSES DEATH

"No one can die unless he chooses death. What seems to be the fear of death is really its attraction. Guilt, too, is feared and fearful. Yet it could have no hold at all except those who are attracted to it and seek it out. And so, it is with death. Made by the ego, its dark shadow falls across all living things, because the ego is 'enemy' of life."

T, 19, C, 1:4-9

THE WORLD IS NOT LEFT BY DEATH BUT BY TRUTH

"The world is not left by death but by truth, and truth can be known by all those for whom the Kingdom was created, and for whom it waits."

T, 3, VII, 6:11

REMEMBER I DID NOT DIE

"When you are tempted to yield to the desire for death, remember that I did not die. You will realize that this is true when you look within and see me. Would I have overcome death for myself alone? And would eternal life have been given me of the Father unless He had also given it to you? When you learn to make me manifest, you will never see death. For you will have looked upon the deathless in yourself, and you will see only the eternal as you look out upon a world that cannot die."

T, 12, VII, 15:1-6

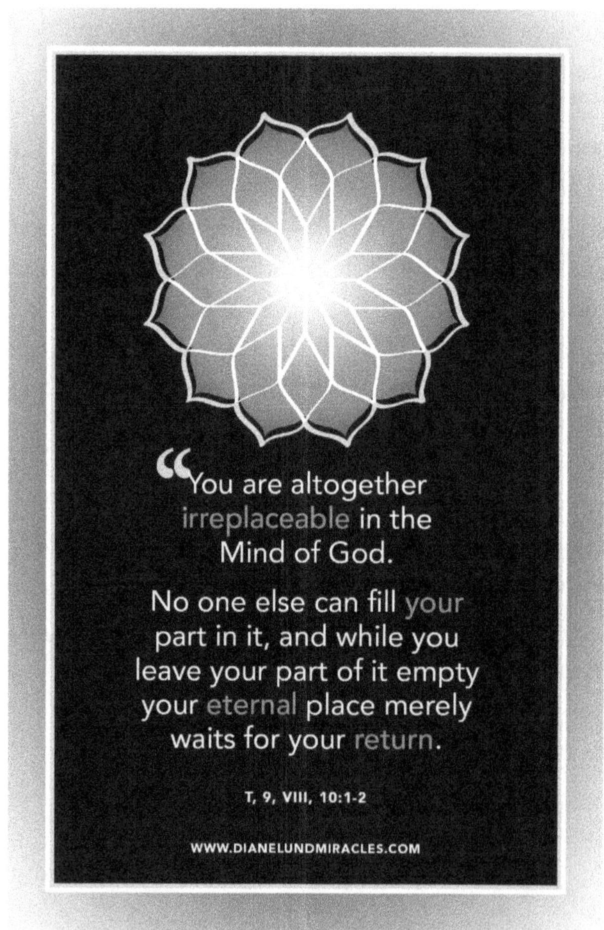

 # Chapter 4

TIME: What Is Time?

Western Thinking
- Time is real.

Reverse Thinking
- Time is an illusion.

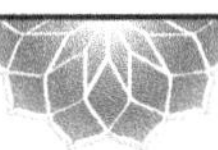

Chapter 4 - Time: What Is Time?
Is there such a thing as perfect timing? Can time be under your control? Watch this video to learn what *A Course in Miracles* teaches us about the subjectivity of time.

http://bit.ly/4TimeWhatIs

TIME IS AN ILLUSION:
MY PERSONAL EXPERIENCE WITH THIS REVERSE THOUGHT

In the physical world, we use time to order our lives. We think in sequential time and create for ourselves a past, present, and future.

We believe time will bring change, which will eventually give us the peace, happiness, and love we desire. Our belief in time, and in the changes it will bring, creates this sequential perception. Without change, there would be no time. This is a condition of spirit; spirit is timeless and eternal.

Think about how you experience time. Everyone has had the experience of doing something that they love and realizing that hours have passed when it felt like mere minutes. Or, perhaps you have had the exact opposite experience: you had to do something you did not enjoy, and so the hours seemed to drag on.
- Can time drag?
- Can time go faster?
- What if time itself is a choice we make in our mind?

I believe time lasts in our mind as long as there are choices to be made. *A Course in Miracles* says:

> *"The purpose of time is to enable you to learn*
> *how to use time constructively.*
> *It is thus a teaching device and a means to an end.*
> *Time will cease when it is no longer useful in facilitating learning."*
>
> T, 1, I, 15:2-4

The following stories are some of my personal experiences with the course's principle about time.

MY DREAM OF TIME
To me, time is a deep and perplexing subject. I believe we understand that best when we are young – time just does not seem to move fast enough. When I went looking for a job in an advertising agency in my early twenties, I did it with organization and passion. I would get out the phone book (no Google in those days) and look up every advertising agency in our city. Then, I would call each agency and ask to speak with their Creative Director. As you can imagine, sometimes I got through to the person and sometimes not. I did manage to get some interviews, but there were no actual job offers. I was told many times by prospective employers that they liked my background and what I had to offer, but there was no job opening at that time. They all said they would call me when there was something concrete. Of course,

I found this frustrating. I kept track of all my calls in a journal. I recorded what people had said, whether I got an interview or not, and what had happened after that. Like a dog tracking a wild scent, I kept my nose down and my enthusiasm for the task high. But days stretched to weeks, and weeks into months, and I was getting desperate and scared that I would not find my ideal job.

One morning I got up, meditated, and then prayed, *Dear God, why am I not getting a job? Why is this taking so long? Please God, help me understand.*

I repeat my questioning prayer over and over again until I was just plain exhausted. So, I lay down on my bed and fell deep asleep.

As I slept, I dreamed I was in a classroom with a big blackboard. In front of the chalkboard stood a teacher who said, *You want to know why? You REALLY want to know why? Well, I will tell you why!* And with that the teacher turned his back and started to write out extremely difficult and hard to understand equations on the blackboard.

The teacher kept talking and writing, talking and writing, until the whole board was covered with equations. Finally, the board was full and the teacher turned around to face me, threw the chalk down on the floor in disgust, and said, *There you go. You wanted to know why: there is the answer.*

The teacher's words and message hit me with such force that they literally knocked me off my feet. In my dream, I fell back onto a bed and immediately appeared to wake up. I sat up on the bed in my dream and looked down at my watch. On the face of the watch were these words:

IT IS NOT THE RIGHT TIME!

I started to laugh and fell back onto my dream bed again.

When I did awaken, I was in my real physical bed. I started to laugh out loud as I remembered,

IT IS NOT THE RIGHT TIME!

The laughing bubbled up from me uncontrollably as I thought about all my insane questioning.

What I seemed to know was this:

TIME IS AN ILLUSION.
I WAS NOT MEANT TO UNDERSTAND IT
AT ITS DEEPEST COSMIC MATHEMATICAL LEVEL.

The overall message of the dream was not confusing to me at the time. I was not getting the job of my dreams because it was not the time for me to get the job of my dreams. This allowed me to **LET GO** and **LET GOD** take care of the timing of things.

YEARS LATER...

I was ready for the next step. I made a commitment to myself to always listen to my inner directive – the small, still voice that always speaks for the right mind and the Holy Spirit. I decided I would not ignore my inner voice anymore, as I had often done in the past. I committed personally and completely to doing whatever my inner voice asked me to do. This was not a decision I took lightly; I was deeply sincere and single-minded in my decision. Here is a story of how this decision affected my life and ended up teaching me more about time.

TIME AND BNI

When a BNI (Business Networking International) chapter was first being created in my area, I decided to check it out. I went to the early morning meeting with a friend, and to say I disliked it would be a vast understatement. It was quite simply everything I did not like. First of all, the meetings started too early. I had to wake up at 5:30 a.m. to get there for 6:30 a.m., and I am not an early bird. Strike one.

Next, I was expected to network with a roomful of strangers. I hated small talk, and the thought of trying to get to know a roomful of people before I had had my coffee was distasteful. Strike two.

Then, I had to stand up and give a one-minute talk about my business in front of these strangers. My heart began pounding out of my chest when I heard that news. *This is so nerve wracking*, I thought. Strike three.

Finally, members were to come every Thursday, every week of the year (or have someone come in their place). I could not believe the level of commitment they were asking for. Are you kidding? Strike four.

When my phone rang early one morning two years later, I heard my inner voice say, *Pick it up!* So, I did, despite my policy to never answer my phone before nine a.m. On the phone was the man who had originally invited me to my first BNI meeting, and he wanted me to give BNI another chance.

"Please," he said, "We think you would be a great addition to our group."

I immediately heard my inner voice say, simply, *Go!*

And, as I had committed to following my inner guidance, I found myself saying, "Okay!"

The moment I hung up the phone, I regretted my answer. I knew I had hated the whole structure of BNI. *Why has my inner voice said to go? That is just so typical,* I thought. I was being asked to go where I did not want to go.

Immediately, fear set in about how early I would have to get up in the morning and all the other things I did not like about BNI.
- I felt fearful of getting up on time.
- I felt fearful of having to stand up and give a speech.
- I felt fearful of meeting so many strangers first thing in the morning.

Hey, my ego voice screamed at me, *You need to get out of this.* And so, my mind started to run crazy with options and ideas.
- I could cancel.
- I could get sick.
- I could sleep in.
- I could just not go.
- I could get an appointment that would take me out of town.

My ego mind was running on fear, and it was having a field day, looking for ways to escape that meeting. I was not happy.

However, over the next few days I reminded myself that my first and primary commitment was to follow the guidance of the Holy Spirit – or my D.I.G. (Divine Inner Guidance), as I often called it. So, I let my ego take its best shot, congratulated it on all its many creative ideas, and went to the meeting anyways.

The day of the meeting, I woke up at 3:00 a.m. and started to worry I would fall asleep and not get up on time. So, I laid awake in bed until 5:30 a.m., at which point I finally got up and got ready to head out. I drove there, parked my car and started to run up the stairs when I heard my little voice say to me, *The man you need will be sitting beside you.*

What? I thought, *I don't need any man. I am married.* And with that I hurried into the meeting.

When I got to the room, the man who invited me said plainly, "You are late!"

What? I thought. *I am ten minutes early according to my timing.*

"I was here at ten after six. You are late!" he said. And with that comment, he whisked me across the room and sat me at a table far away from where he was seated.

Of all the nerve! I thought my ego grumbling along with me. *What a jerk. I can't believe I got up this early to get treated so rudely. I really do not know what I am doing here!*

I was so mad and caught up in my own thoughts that I did not pay any attention to who was seated next to me. However, when the time came to deliver our personal talk about our business, the man stood up and talked about tires. I just about fell off my seat in disbelief when I heard that – I had been looking for tires all week. My inner voice had been right: *The man you need will be sitting beside you.* How extraordinary! My inner guidance cares about me, right down to my tire selection.

This event made me decide there was something beyond me that certainly wanted me to attend BNI, so I followed my inner voice and joined the group. I want to note that this does not mean I wanted to join; in fact I hated every early morning. Over and over I asked, *Why BNI? What am I supposed to be learning?*

I did not get a clear answer right away. In fact, it was months of asking before I clearly heard within, *You think time is real. We are teaching you about the illusion of time through BNI. There is really no good time or bad time – you are making these illusions real. We are helping you examine them.*

Of all the crazy answers! Truly, I had expected to hear something like the following:
- We need you to help people.
- We are addressing your fear of facing a room full of strangers.
- We are helping you become a better public speaker.

I never expected to hear, *We are teaching you about time. You think it is real. We are helping you learn it is not real. It is an illusion. Your trouble with time is all in your head.*

Your inner guide knows what you need to learn.

I did not know I needed to address my issues with time! I don't think it was even on my radar – I thought I just knew what I liked and what I did not like. Herein lies a clue. Often, what we resist holds the seeds of our next growth, and so what we think we need to learn may not be what our spirit or soul truly needs to address.

After hearing that information from my inner guidance, I started to look at how time runs my life. Here were some of my thoughts.

- *I have a time I like to get up in the morning.*
- *I have an idea about when it is a good time to talk to people about sensitive things and when it is not.*
- *I have lots of time for work and little time for play.*
- *I have time for others but little time for myself.*
- *I worry about being late for others or being on time for my husband. He hates arriving late.*

As I examined these thoughts, I started to realize that it was true: time was running my life.

BNI was one way I started to face my time issues. I started to get up at a time I did not like, and slowly but surely I learned that I could like that time just as much as any other. In fact, I started to see sunrises that were spectacular, and I loved having put in hours of networking and building my business before I even got to work. Best of all, when I was going to Nashville and the first leg of the flight left for Los Angeles at 6:00 a.m. – which meant I needed to get up at 2:00 a.m. – I surprised myself when I did not hate getting up at this time. In fact, I rather enjoyed the challenge of it, and I was thrilled when I was in Nashville by the afternoon, with enough time to go for a swim!

I began to see time is an illusion I am creating with my mind and so I began to ask myself certain questions:

- *Is there really a good time or a bad time for anything?*
- *Can you really be late, or are you always exactly on time?*

Today, I no longer believe there is a good time and a bad time. I no longer believe anyone is late. I see myself and everyone else as being perfectly on time – whatever time it is. Now I believe:

- Time is a construct of the mind.
- Think about it – you have never been anywhere but the present.
- There really is no past and no future except in your mind. The past and the future actually do not exist.
- You are always only living in the present, in the eternal now. This is the truth.
- The only time there has ever been is NOW.

Through listening to my inner voice, I have taught myself that time is an illusion. I do not believe I have this principle down pat, but I am open to listening to the Voice for God within. I believe my Divine Inner Guidance understands things well beyond my conscious understanding, as demonstrated to me both by my dream of time and by my experiences of time through BNI.

How divine!

WHAT DOES *A COURSE IN MIRACLES* SAY ABOUT TIME?

Here on the physical plane, we mark our days with time. We mark our history with time. We order our physical world with time. However, time is a concept that is in direct contrast to eternity. God's world is eternal. There is no time; there is only the present.

When we acknowledge to ourselves that all we have ever had and will ever have is available right now, we no longer put our lives on hold waiting for the future. Everything exists in the now. This should be good news – if you do not feel you have everything you desire, perhaps it is because you do not acknowledge that it is possible to have it now. Perhaps you believe it is too difficult.

Whatever you believe, you are right. You project your thoughts out into the cosmos, and the cosmos manifests what you believe right in front of your eyes. If you believe now is not a good time, it will not be a good time. If you believe you have to wait and pay your dues, you will have to wait and pay your dues. Time is plastic or fluid – it bends and conforms to what we think. Most of us believe it is linear and cannot be altered, but do you really know that this is the truth?

> *"The basic decision of the miracle-minded*
> *is not to wait on time any longer than is necessary.*
> *Time can waste as well as be wasted.*
> *The miracle worker, therefore, accepts the time-control factor gladly.*
> *He recognizes that every collapse of time brings everyone closer to the ultimate release from time,*
> *in which the Son and the Father are one."*
>
> T, 1, V, 2:2-4

Perhaps it is time to play with our idea of time.
- What if this was the best time ever to do all you ever wanted?
- What would you do with your time now?

A Course in Miracles says that when we think from love and extend that love, miracles happen which can collapse time. What an amazing thought!

LET THE FUTURE GO, AND PLACE IT IN GOD'S HANDS

"God holds your future as He holds your past and present. They are one to Him, and so they should be one to you. Yet in this world, the temporal progression still seems real. And so, you are not asked to understand the lack of sequence really found in time. You are but asked to the let the future go, and place it in God's hands."

W, L194, 4:1-5

TIME IS YOUR FRIEND

"Time is your friend, if you leave it to the Holy Spirit to use. He needs but very little to restore God's whole power to you. He who transcends time for you understands what time is for. Holiness lies not in time, but in eternity."

T, 15, I, 15:1-4

TIME ITSELF IS YOUR CHOICE

"Time itself is your choice. If you would remember eternity, you must look only on the eternal. If you allow yourself to become preoccupied with the temporal, you are living in time. As always, your choice is determined by what you value. Time and eternity cannot both be real, because they contradict each other. If you will accept only what is timeless as real, you will begin to understand eternity and make it yours."

T, 10, V, 14:4-9

TIME AND TIMELESSNESS

"Time is under my direction, but timelessness belongs to God. In time, we exist for and with each other. In timelessness we coexist with God."

T, 2, V, 17:5-6

TIME IS A MEANS TO REGAIN ETERNITY

"Time and eternity are both in your mind, and will conflict until you perceive time solely as a means to regain eternity."

T, 10, Introduction, 1:2

THE ONLY ASPECT OF TIME THAT IS ETERNAL IS NOW

"Time is a belief of the ego, so the lower mind, which is the ego's domain, accepts it without question. The only aspect of time that is eternal is now."

T, 5, III, 6:4-5

TIME IS A LEARNING DEVICE

"We have repeatedly said that time is a learning device to be abolished when it is no longer useful."

T, 5, VI, 12:4

TIME CAN NEVER TAKE AWAY A VALUE THAT IS REAL

"Time can never take away a value that is real. What fades and dies was never there, and makes no offering to him who chooses it."

W, L133, 6:3-4

WHY WAIT FOR HEAVEN?
IT IS HERE TODAY

Why wait for Heaven? It is here today. Time is the great illusion it is past or in the future. Yet this cannot be, if it is where God wills His Son to be. How could the Will of God be in the past, or yet to happen? What He wills is now, without a past and wholly futureless. It is as far removed from time as is a tiny candle from a distant star, or what you chose from you really want."

W, L131, 6:1-7

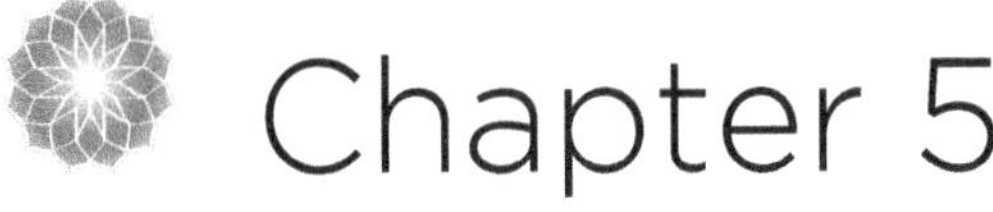# Chapter 5

REALITY: What Is Real?

Western Thinking
- The physical world is real.

Reverse Thinking
- The physical world is an illusion.

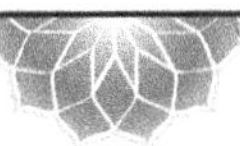

Chapter 5 - Reality: What Is Real?
Watch this video to learn the one thing that is truly real and lasting versus what is illusory, according to *A Course in Miracles.*

http://bit.ly/5Reality

THE PHYSICAL WORLD IS AN ILLUSION:
MY PERSONAL EXPERIENCE WITH THIS REVERSE THOUGHT

Generally, the physical world teaches us that what we can touch, see, hear, taste, and smell is real. We rely on our five physical senses to perceive our world, and we are raised to believe the information these senses relay to us is true and real. For example, we pick up a glass, and we believe this is a glass. If someone asked us, "Is this glass real?" most of us would say that it was. But what if I took that glass, smashed it into pieces, heated the pieces, and made a mirror. Now the question I ask is, "Is this a glass, or is it a mirror, or is it both?" It appears the glass has changed from one thing to another.

A Course in Miracles says the physical world is not real because everything within the physical world shifts and changes, like a glass becoming a mirror or water evaporating and becoming clouds. According to the course, the physical world is unreal because it shifts and changes. It is an ever-changing illusion.

WHAT IS REAL AND WHAT IS UNREAL?

The definition of what is real and what is unreal is central to the course. To understand this concept, let's look at the weather. You might look out your window and say, "It looks like it is a rainy day." Later, you walk outside and feel the rain on your head as you run for shelter into an airport. In the plane a few hours later, you rise through the clouds and there it is – a totally sunny day.

The fact is that the sun did not go away because you saw a rainy day.
What happened was clouds covered the sun, and you decided – based on the information your eyes told you – that it was a dark, gloomy, rainy day. However, it was also a totally sunny day above the clouds. From this example, we can see that there is no ultimate physical reality. What we perceive really just depends on your perspective and your location in space and time. We can use this same metaphor to understand what happens to us. Within each of us there is an inner, eternal light. When we take on a human form, this inner light is covered over by flesh and bones – like the clouds covering up the sun. When we look at each other, we do not see radiant light. Instead, we see a physical body.

Does this mean that the inner radiance has gone away or does not exist?
With our physical eyes, we cannot see our inner radiance. But, does that mean it is not there? *A Course in Miracles* differentiates between eyesight and spiritual sight, and it reminds us of something truly amazing.

We all see with our eyes closed!
Think about it. At night, when we close our eyes and go to sleep, we dream. In these dreams, we all see images, places, and people. But have you ever stopped to ask yourself, *What is seeing the images?* I am sure we can all agree it is not our physical eyes, since our eyes are closed.

Could it be that we have inner vision that does not rely on physical eyesight?

It certainly appears so to me. I have vivid, clear dreams full of sight, sound, colour, and feeling. However, when I open my eyes, the images vanish. So for me, the question once again emerges: what is real, and what is not?

- Are my dreams real or unreal?
- Can I trust what my physical senses tell me to be the ultimate truth?

Here's an interesting story I read about eyesight that can illuminate how this sense works.

CAN A BLIND MAN SEE?

There is a fascinating book about a man who lost his sight when he was five after a chemical explosion. In his forties, he had the opportunity to have his eyesight restored through a stem cell operation. This is the true story of Mike May, a three-time Paralympic gold medalist, entrepreneur, husband, and loving father. Mike was not interested in the procedure at first as he loved his life, but his curiosity eventually overcame him and he underwent the surgery to repair his cornea.

This operation turned out to be just the beginning of Mike's journey. He and his doctors learned sight has more to do with the mind than just the physical condition of the eyes.

The operation did give Mike brand new corneas, but they did not allow Mike to see. He had learned since the age of five to "see" the world through touch and sound. Now, with the new corneas in place, he saw shadowy images that he did not understand. The doctors and Mike learned that perfect corneas do not enable perfect vision. In the end, they learned **it is not the physical eyes that see – it is the mind's interpretation of what it sees that allows you to have vision.**

This story is well documented in the book *Crashing Through: A True Story of Risk, Adventure and the Man Who Dared to See* by Robert Kurson. I highly recommend reading it if you are interested in learning about how our eyesight is something that we train our minds to do. I believe we cannot see things the mind cannot conceive of.

Does that mean that what we do not see does not exist?

Of course not. We do not see radio waves, nor do we see the electromagnetic waves that allow us to use our televisions and cell phones. So, although a common Western belief is that what is visible to our eyes exists and is real – and conversely, what is invisible to our eyes does not exist and is unreal – we can safely say this absolutely cannot be true.

Every day, your world is powered by things you cannot see: your television, your cell phone, your cordless phone, and your satellite radio. And yet people still deny that the invisible realm is real; in turn, this leads them to deny their inner sight. They insist their inner vision or internal spiritual sight is unreal and does not exist.

A Course in Miracles asks us to turn this concept upside down. It does not rely on physical sight to determine if something is real or not. Instead, it changes up the game and claims what is real is anything that never changes, and what is unreal is anything that does change. So, what would that be exactly?

SOMETHING THAT NEVER CHANGES IS LOVE
According to *A Course in Miracles*, something that never changes is love. Love is the same today as it was hundreds of years ago, and it will be the same five hundred years from now. Love is also invisible, yet most of us would argue that it certainly does exist. We feel love. This inner, eternal love is often called your spirit. So, according to *A Course in Miracles*, spirit/love is real because it is eternal and never changes.

SOMETHING THAT ALWAYS CHANGES IS THE PHYSICAL BODY
I am sure we will all agree that we do not look the same at five years old as we do at twenty-five years old, or at fifty-five. Our body changes, and what you could do yesterday you may not be able to do today. Our abilities and physical strength come and go, and ultimately, the body itself comes and goes. So, according to *A Course in Miracles,* the physical body is unreal or an illusion because it is in a constant state of change.

IN SUMMARY
The spirit or eternal love inside of you (which you cannot see) is real because it does not change. The physical body (which you can see) that constantly changes and dies is (according to *A Course in Miracles*) unreal. Okay, that is a 180-degree turn around in thinking for most people. That's what I call reverse thinking!

WHAT DOES *A COURSE IN MIRACLES* SAY ABOUT WHAT IS REAL?

If our spirit is real and our body is unreal, where does that leave us? Does that mean that we should ignore the physical world and just think of ourselves as love or spirit? I do not think it makes any sense to ignore the body – even *A Course in Miracles* says we are here in physical form, and it would be silly to ignore this fact.

> *"The body is merely part of your experience in the physical world.*
> *Its abilities can be and frequently are over evaluated.*
> *However, it is almost impossible to deny its existence in this world.*
> *Those who do so are engaging in a particularly unworthy form of denial."*
> T, 2, VI, 3:8-11

A Course in Miracles says our bodies are to be used as communication vehicles for the spirit. Instead of seeing just the physical world and believing it is real, perhaps it is time to develop our inner, intuitive senses.

> *"Corrective learning always begins with the awakening of spirit,*
> *and the turning away from the belief in physical sight.*
> *This often entails fear, because you are afraid*
> *of what your spiritual sight will show you."*
> T, 2, V, 7:1-2

What we see in form is never the ultimate reality, because it is always changing. All physical form is an illusion, and to put your faith in a changing illusion brings pain. What we can put our faith in is what is eternal, and this reality is literally built in to each of us. It is our spirit. It is invisible, but we can feel it, know it, and learn to have faith in it through our experiences and practises.

What if your body is not your ultimate reality? What if it is just a tool we use to help us get in touch with our inner spiritual reality, where love abides eternally? Perhaps it is time to develop and strengthen our inner, intuitive senses – spiritual sight, inner hearing, and inner knowing – to access what is in fact real: eternal love. *A Course in Miracles* says that you can use these inner faculties to find your true path home; all you need is a little willingness to try. You can start by looking at these quotes from *A Course in Miracles*. Can you open your mind to embrace the ideas presented?

NOTHING REAL CAN BE THREATENED

"Nothing real can be threatened. Nothing unreal exists.
Herein lies the peace of God."

T, Introduction 2:1-4

REALITY BELONGS ONLY TO SPIRIT

"Reality belongs only to spirit, and the miracle acknowledges this truth. It thus dispels illusions about yourself, and puts you in communion with yourself and God."

T, I, IV, 2:4-5

DENIAL OF SPIRITUAL SIGHT

"You believe that what physical eyes cannot see does not exist. This leads to the denial of spiritual sight."

T, 1, I, 22:2-3

A MADMAN THINKS THE WORLD HE SEES IS REAL

"The thoughts you hold are mighty, and illusions are as strong in their effects as is the truth. A madman thinks the world he sees is real, and does not doubt it. Nor can he be swayed by questioning his thoughts' effects. It is but when their source is raised to question that the hope of freedom comes to him at last."

W, L132, 1:4-7

THERE IS NO WORLD

"There is no world because it is a thought apart from God, and made to separate the Father and the Son, and break away a part of God Himself and thus destroy His Wholeness. Can a world that comes from this idea be real?"

W, L132, 13:1-2

SPIRITUAL VISION LITERALLY CANNOT SEE ERROR

"Spiritual vision literally cannot see error, and merely looks for Atonement. All solutions the physical eye seeks dissolve. Spiritual vision looks within and recognizes immediately that the altar has been defiled and needs to be repaired and protected. Perfectly aware of the right defense it passes over all others, looking past error to truth."

T, 2, III, 4:1-4

WHAT THE PHYSICAL EYE SEES IS NOT CORRECTIVE

"What the physical eye sees is not corrective, nor can error be corrected by any device that can be seen physically. As long as you believe in what your physical sight tells you, your attempts at correction will be misdirected. The real vision is obscured, because you cannot endure to see your own defiled altar."

T, 2, V, 8:2-4

YOU CANNOT SEE APART FROM GOD

"You cannot see apart from God because you cannot be apart from God. Whatever you do you do in Him, because whatever you think, you think with His Mind. If vision is real, and it is real to the extent to which it shares the Holy Spirit's purpose, then you cannot see apart from God."

W, L43, 3:1-3

THERE IS ANOTHER WAY OF LOOKING AT THE WORLD

"Since the purpose of the world is not the one I ascribed to it, there must be another way of looking at it. I see everything upside down, and my thoughts are the opposite of truth. I see the world as a prison for God's Son. It must be, then, that the world is really a place where he can be set free. I would look upon the world as it is, and see it as a place the Son of God finds his freedom."

W, L57, 3:(33):1-6

PART TWO

RELATIONSHIPS:
Every Relationship
Is a Lesson in Love

*"Under His teaching, every relationship
becomes a lesson in love."*

T, 15, V, 4:6

INTRODUCTION

WHERE IS LOVE?

The whole world is searching for love. We all want it. We all need it. And that's the problem: we don't recognize that we *are* it. We are love, so we cannot lose it. Love isn't a thing that can be lost and found. But we can forget about it and block it from our minds, and that is literally what we have done and continue to do.

We block love from entering our conscious minds. How do we do that? We focus on fear. Our minds and our thinking are all tied up with fearful thoughts. We all know the lonely refrains of our ego thoughts. It goes something like this:

> *The last person I loved hurt me.*
> *I gave everything I had to that last relationship,*
> *and I am still hurting.*
> *Love hurts.*
> *Love is painful.*

The fact is, love is not painful; it just is. Instead, it is our thinking about love that is paining us!
- Love just is.
- It always exists.
- It does not change or alter.

However we decide whether or not we will let the light of love into our thinking. The fact that we go searching for it innately says that we don't believe we have it. And in this way of thinking, we align with the ego's thought system. Or, to put it another way, our thinking is based on fearful thoughts.

Real love, according to the course, is the absence of fear, because love is complete and whole and asks nothing from anyone or anything. Consequently, it is a whole or holy state of mind. According to *A Course in Miracles*, this state of mind recognizes the authority of God so completely that it relinquishes all psychological attachment to anything that is not God.
- Anything that comes from God must be exactly like God.
- God is perfect and eternal.

So, it follows that you must also be perfect and eternal. To think this way, you must realize you do not get to decide what you are – God decides what you are. If you think you are "stupid" or "incomplete," you have decided you are the author of what is, which means you are basically telling God what to think of you. This is really arrogant, according to the course. To side with and for God, you must be willing to give up the authorship of your life to He who truly knows who you are. True humility is the way. Here's how *A Course in Miracles* talks about this concept:

*"Today we practice true humility,
abandoning the false pretense by which the ego seeks to prove it arrogant.
Only the ego can be arrogant.
But truth is humble in acknowledging its mightiness,
its changelessness and its eternal wholeness,
all-encompassing, God's perfect gift to His beloved Son.
We lay aside the arrogance which says that we are sinners,
guilty and afraid, ashamed of what we are;
and lift our hearts in true humility instead to Him
Who has created us immaculate, like to Himself in power and in love."*
W, L152, 9:1-4

SPECIAL LOVES

Most of our physical expressions of love here on the physical plane are what the course calls **special love**. This state of mind creates idols. We judge a person as "special," as having what we want, and so we idolize them. Then we want that person to like us, accept us, live with us, marry us, love us – whatever form fits our fantasy. Underneath these fantasy thoughts, we believe we are incomplete, and that we need this special person to help make our lives complete. In short, we believe our personal special needs are to be met by special people with special attributes. We call this love. The course calls this **special love**, because it is all about getting something from someone that we think we need.

What we are forgetting is that real love is NOT needy. Special love is needy. Special love takes one person and splits them away from the whole. It says, this one person is it! They are the love I need. And if we feel this love is not returned to us, we make ourselves unhappy.

Special love suggests that we are not whole, and that someone else will have something that will fill us up and make us happy. This needy type of love can be strangling to another person because deep within ourselves, we all know we can never fulfill someone else. Most of us cannot even make ourselves happy, let alone another person! This awareness may not be conscious, but it is the reason we run from clinging and needy relationships. Deep down, we know we cannot be their saviours, and we do not want the job. We know we will fail, and then the relationship may turn ugly. It may turn into a **special hate**.

SPECIAL HATES

This state of mind creates enemies. We judge some people as not having what we want and we do not see their behaviour as loving. Instead, we feel like we are attacked, criticized, not seen or not appreciated – pick one or many. So, we decide this is a person and an experience we do not like. In fact, we often hate the person. We confuse the person with the behaviour, and we create **special hates**.

Most people know love gone wrong. People who married and pledged to love one another are suddenly at each other's throats, arguing over possessions, children, pets, and money. People we love become people we love to hate. This is never pretty, nor fun, and it is why many people shy away from relationships. If we don't deliver what a person wants from us, we are suddenly the enemy. Oh, how quickly special love can turn to special hate. It all sounds depressing, but it is all too accurate. How can we turn these situations around? How can we get the love we desire?

Here are a couple of thoughts that may help:
- All relationships are assignments.
- All relationships are really lessons in love.
- We can choose to have a Special Relationship or a Holy Relationship.

WHAT IS A HOLY RELATIONSHIP?

Relationships are about learning to see others as perfect love. Anytime you meet someone, *A Course in Miracles* says to remember it is a holy encounter. What is that? A holy encounter is when we choose to see the other person as part of ourselves, as being one in spirit.

The course says that as you see your brother or sister, so will you see yourself. As you treat him/her, so will you treat yourself. And as you think of him/her, so will you think of yourself. It implores us to never forget this, for in this you will find yourself or lose yourself.

"God's Teacher speaks to any two who join together for learning purposes.
The relationship is holy because of that purpose,
and God has promised to send His Spirit into any holy relationship.
In the teaching-learning situation,
each one learns that giving and receiving are the same.
The demarcations they have drawn between
their roles, their minds, their bodies, their needs, their interests, and all the differences they thought
separated them from one another,
fade and grow dim and disappear."

M, 2, 5:3-6

WHAT HAVE WE FORGOTTEN THAT WE REALLY NEED TO KNOW?

Our brothers, sisters, family, and children are a bridge to the divine. In order to experience joy and love, we need to show up in relationships:

- whole,
- letting things be, and
- appreciating what is.

We block the awareness of love's presence when we look to others and not ourselves for fulfillment. We block the awareness of love's presence when we blame others for our problems. We are here to share, support, and care for each other, not to demand, insist, and criticize others when they are not showing up the way we want them to show up for us.

WHERE DOES IT ALL GO WRONG?

It all goes wrong in the mind. We see a lack in ourselves. We want to find someone to fill the lack we feel inside, as a relationship seems to fulfill our needs. This often happens for a time. For example, in romantic love, the partner appears to be what we are looking for until time passes and we learn things about our partner that we do not like or want. They are no longer ALL we imagined them to be (romantic love is what we imagine or want other people to be for us). Instead, they show up as they are. Our fantasy of the other person is unravelling. When that happens, we often:

- fight,
- accuse,
- play the victim,
- manipulate,
- leave,
- avoid,
- abuse,
- hate,
- cry,
- scream,
- have a fit,
- go to fear,
- overeat,
- overdrink or
- run away.

Pick one. Or, pick a few – we usually do.

The following chapter looks at some of the ways the Western world traditionally looks at love and how *A Course in Miracles* principles can turn that thinking 180-degrees, helping you go from hurt and pain to love and joy within your relationships.

Remember, every relationship is a lesson in love.

 # Chapter 6

LOVE: Where Is Love?

Western Thinking
- I need to find love.

Reverse Thinking
- I am love.

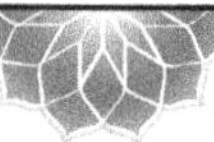

Chapter 6 - Love: Where Is Love?
Can love be found? Everyone wants love in his or her life. We often go in search of it. But, that's looking for love in all the wrong places. Watch this video to learn what *A Course in Miracles* teaches us about searching for love.

http://bit.ly/6LoveWhere

I AM LOVE:
MY PERSONAL EXPERIENCE WITH THIS REVERSE THOUGHT

My own personal journey to the awareness of love's presence in all things has been a long and winding one. Growing up in a family of alcoholics, I often did not feel loved. Instead, I felt left out and alone. My parents were all wrapped up in their fighting, their addictions, and their problems. I was told, "Children are to be seen and not heard!" I am sure many people can relate to that experience.

I went looking for love because it didn't seem to be consistently present in my home life, in my parents relationship with each other, or in their relationship with us. Love at home was a kind of on-again-off-again feeling. Worst of all, I never knew which days it would be on and which days it would be off.

I walked on eggshells around my parents, looking for their approval, but nothing I did ever seemed to be enough. When I got straight A's, my mother hid my report card under the dishcloths in a drawer. "Let's not show that to your sisters," she would say. In contrast, my sister, who got mid-range grades, had her report card taped up on the fridge door. I was told to praise my sister for how well she had done, which left me confused. My good grades were being hidden while my sister's average grades were getting applauded. Years later I realize what my mom was trying to do, but I didn't understand it at the time. I thought I had to try harder, and that what I had done was not good enough. I internalized it all and concluded in my young mind that I was not loved, or possibly that I was not loveable. My answer: I needed to get out of there and find love.

Love became my drug of choice. In my teen years, I wanted my boyfriend to love me, my friends to love me, my teachers to love me. I was looking outside of myself for love in all the wrong places. And of course, you know what happened. When you locate love in people and things outside of yourself, you give away your power. You ultimately declare (although unconsciously), *I am not love. I need love to come from this person or this thing.* And with that, you give away your sense of control. You are at the mercy of the object of your affection showing up or not showing up for you. This was my story for many, many years.

MY SPECIAL LOVE
In Grade Nine, I looked across the gym floor and spotted him: my special love.

How did I know, you ask? I just knew. I knew in my heart, not in my head. However, I was shy. I told my girlfriends about my crush, and they immediately went to work. They found out his name and told his friends about my feelings. I was mortified, but also secretly glad. After all, I was not going to go and talk to him; I was fifteen years old and scared of boys. I had a mom, two sisters, and a dad that was seldom at home. I knew girls, but boys were a mystery to me.

Eventually, my crush and I were introduced, and we started to see each other on the school grounds. We sat in the bleachers and ate lunch together and we took walks at noon hour. After a month or so, we decided to go on a date on a Sunday afternoon.

Well, the day of the date came, and I was too scared to go. I sat at home and looked out my window, wishing I had the nerve to go and meet him. He came to me the next day at school, hurt and wondering what had happened to me. I told him I was too scared to go out to meet him. He was very understanding, and that helped us to get closer. Eventually, he asked me to go out with him. I still remember the day – I was so happy. We had our first kiss outside of the library a couple of months later.

We continued to date all the way through high school, but I refused to sleep with him. My mom said we were far too young, and that sex confuses everything. Of course, I believed her. I remember telling him that if he wanted sex, he was going to have to look elsewhere. I would turn a blind eye. This opened the door for him to see other people behind my back, but I thought that was okay because I was not going to deliver all that he wanted from me.

Summers were a lonely time. My boyfriend went away to camp to be a counsellor, so I was left without him for the whole summer. I remember learning to not like the summers – while I was sitting home alone, everyone else was going to beach parties and hanging out in couples. I felt isolated and lonely.

I was a year older than my boyfriend, which meant I graduated a year before him. Being in different grades was difficult because we were often going through different experiences. I was going off to university, and I thought that meant I needed to see the world. I needed to be free to have new experiences. I wanted to date people in the summer, not just sit around and wait for him. So, the on-again-off-again part of our relationship began. I knew I needed new experiences to grow and understand life, but I took him seriously when he said, "We will marry when we are twenty-seven." I sure hoped so. In fact, I pinned my happiness on the belief that eventually we would be together.

But twenty-seven came and went and although we were seeing each other now and again, there was no proposal. In fact, I heard that there were other women, and perhaps even other men. I felt hurt, but I did not give up! I understood I had opened that door a long time ago. And somewhere deep down I felt responsible for his straying behaviour, even though we were now a couple that slept together.

Then came the moment when I learned without a doubt that he was seeing someone else while he was seeing me. He thought it was no big deal since this was our history together, and he was right. He had always been seeing other people. I think I always knew this, but the hard-core reality of it sank deep into my heart as his words rang in my ears. If I wanted to be with this person, affairs and deception were going to be part of the package. There was no denying the truth. I had set up this dynamic years ago by turning a blind eye when we were young, but now things were different. We were older, but perhaps not any wiser.

This type of relationship was deeply painful for me, and there was no hiding from the pain. So, I decided to do the one thing I never wanted to do – I needed to draw a line in the sand. I needed to stand up for what I knew I wanted in my heart: a loving, committed relationship, not a relationship where there were other people in the mix. I made the painful decision and told him, "I let you go completely."

He was in disbelief. "But, this is what we do," he said.

"Not anymore," I replied in all seriousness.

I was letting go of a man I deeply and truly loved. I wanted him more than anything, but I suspected I wanted him for the wrong reasons. I wanted him to make me happy. I knew it was the wrong motivation, so I honoured my truth and we parted ways.

IT WAS NOT A HAPPY ENDING

We never got back together. I have never stopped loving him, but I know in my heart that letting him go was the biggest loving act of my life. He obviously did not want to live the way I wanted to live, and that was his right. It was not up to me to change him, or catch him, or anything like that. It was up to me to honour who he was, and to let him find himself and his way. I knew he did not want the responsibility of a committed relationship but I did. We were simply standing in two different places.

I wish I could tell you that the pain of that break up went away, but it did not dull for many, many years. Deep in my heart, I always felt tied to that person. What helped was knowing we were always together in spirit, even though we were not physically together.

My deep learning from this relationship was:
- Real love does not possess.
- Real love does not need.
- Real love is whole and complete and needs nothing from the other.

I knew this was the truth, but it was painful to let go and not get what I wanted. However, in my heart and soul, I knew it was the right thing to do.

I am now happy to report that many, many years later, I eventually did get to the point where I could have a relationship that was not based on need. I found my own loving centre, and because of that, I no longer needed someone to fill the hole within – but that's another chapter.

WHAT I KNOW FOR SURE

Today, I know one thing for sure: real love never changes.

- Love is.
- Love is your natural inheritance.
- Love is what you are eternally.

This cannot be taught; it must be experienced.

The course puts this elegantly in its opening Introduction:

"The course does not aim at teaching the meaning of love,
for that is beyond what can be taught.
It does aim, however,
at removing the blocks to the awareness of love's presence,
which is your natural inheritance."

T, Introduction: 1:6-7

A Course In Miracles is really about teaching us how to remove the blocks to our awareness of love's presence in our individual lives.

Love just is, and we cannot change that. It is the fabric of the cosmos, and it is what binds the world and our worlds together. However, we can block love and deny its reality in our lives. We can point out all the ways we are victimized, left alone, left out, and ignored. We keep true love separated or walled off from ourselves, and the ways we do this are bountiful. We often:

- defend,
- fight,
- run away,
- hold ourselves apart,
- reject people,
- attack,
- judge,
- condemn,
- sabotage,
- avoid,
- blame,
- punish,
- criticize,

- abandon,
- expect, and
- withhold.

Let's face it, this list can go on and on. Everyone picks and chooses a personal blend of negative reactions to use. Real, authentic love patiently waits deep within each and every one of us, but we resist, afraid that if we allow ourselves to feel the love, then that love will be withdrawn and we will be left with hurt, betrayal, and pain.

In our physical universe, there is no denying that this fear is real. People are killed, children die, lovers cheat and countries go to war. But the fact remains the same: love is, because love is not exclusively in a person, place, or thing. It cannot be captured, held down, married, divorced, or uprooted.

- Love is your natural inheritance.
- It is who you truly are in your spirit.

Once you experience yourself as love – once you embrace yourself as love – you will see the world through love's eyes. And this shift in perception is what the course calls a miracle.

WHAT DOES *A COURSE IN MIRACLES* SAY ABOUT LOVE?

The course divides the topic of love into three parts: special love relationships, special hate relationships, and holy relationships. Whenever you desire to get something from someone else in a love relationship, you believe you are not whole, and that you are missing something that someone else possesses. When you do this, you are not in alignment with God's knowledge of you.

According to *A Course in Miracles,* we were all created by God's extension of whole, perfect love – therefore, you cannot be anything but love. So, when you go looking for love, you are not realizing, that you already have love, because you are love. Once you embrace this idea fully, you are then in the position to give love. You see, you cannot give something you do not possess. So, our task is not to seek love, but merely to find all the barriers we have built against it.

Fear, anger, jealousy, resentment, unhappiness, depression, and anxiety – these are just some of the feelings that lock out our awareness of love. Special love relationships and special hate relationships bring these feelings to the forefront of our mind, and being aware of these feelings is often the first step. Once we acknowledge that we have these feelings, we have the opportunity to change our minds. For example, if we remember that everyone came from the extension of God's love, then we could acknowledge they are love. They are not a monster or a hero in our life. Their true, authentic nature is love, and if they are not showing you this aspect of themselves, it is because they have forgotten this truth. The course says that when your partner or friend has truly forgotten who they are, it is your opportunity to remember it for them. Forgive their behaviour. See the love under the surface. As you release your brother or your sister, so you will be released. This is a miracle in the course's definition, and is why relationships are the foundation of our learning here on earth. We cannot do this alone. When we decide together to use our relationships to purify our mind, we enter into a holy relationship.

FOR GOD CREATED LOVE
"For God created love as He would have it be, and gave it as it is. Love has no meaning except as its Creator defined it by His Will. It is impossible to define it otherwise and understand it."

T, 16, VI, 1:6-7

LOVE IS NOT AN ILLUSION. IT IS A FACT.
"Love is not an illusion. It is a fact. Where disillusionment is possible, there was not love but hate. For hate is an illusion and what can change was never love."

T, 16, IV, 4:1-4

IF YOU SEEK LOVE OUTSIDE OF YOURSELF

"If you seek love outside yourself you can be certain that you perceive hatred within, and are afraid of it. Yet peace will never come from the illusion of love, but only from its reality."

T, 16, IV, 6:1-2

LOVE ENTERS ANY MIND THAT TRULY WANTS IT

"Love will immediately enter into any mind that truly wants it, but it must want it truly."

T, 4, III, 4:7

LOVE IS EXTENSION

"Love is extension. To withhold the smallest gift is not to know love's purpose. Love offers everything forever. Hold back but one belief, one offering, and love is gone, because you asked a substitute to take its place."

T, 24, I, 1:1-4

LOVE DOES NOT COMPARE

"Love makes no comparisons. And gratitude can only be sincere if it be joined to love."

W, L195, 4:2-3

LOVE IS NOT SPECIAL

"Love is not special. If you single out part of the Sonship for your love, you are imposing guilt on all your relationships and making them unreal. You can love only as God loves."

T, 13, X, 11:2-4

DON'T BE AFRAID OF LOVE

"Be not afraid of love. For it alone can heal all sorrow, wipe away all tears, and gently waken from his dream of pain the Son whom God acknowledges as His. Be not afraid of this. Salvation asks you give it welcome. And the world awaits your glad acceptance, which will set it free."

W, L310, 4:2-6

LOVE'S ARMS ARE OPEN

"Love's arms are open to receive you, and give you peace forever."

T, 20, VI, 10:6

LOVE IS FREEDOM

"Love is freedom."

T, 16, VI, 2:1

LOVE WISHES TO BE KNOWN

"Love wishes to be known, completely understood and shared. It has no secrets; nothing that it would keep apart and hide. It walks in sunlight, open-eyed and calm, in smiling welcome and in sincerity so simple and so obvious it cannot be misunderstood."

T, 20, VI, 2:5-7

LOVE DOES NOT KILL TO SAVE

"They seem to love, yet they desert, and are deserted. They appear to lose what they love, perhaps the most insane belief of all. And their bodies wither and gasp and are laid in the ground, and are no more. Not one of them but has thought that God is cruel."

T, 13, Introduction, 2:8-10

"If this were the real world, God would be cruel. For no Father could subject His children to this as the price of salvation and be loving. Love does not kill to save."

T, 13, Introduction, 3:1-3

MAKE WAY FOR LOVE

"Make way for love, which you did not create, but which you can extend. On earth this means forgive your brother, that the darkness may be lifted from your mind. When light has come to him through your forgiveness, he will not forget his savior, leaving him unsaved. For it was in your face he saw the light that he would keep beside him, as he walks through darkness to the everlasting light."

T, 29, III, 4:1-4

PERFECT LOVE IS IN YOU!

"You have so little faith in yourself because you are unwilling to accept the fact that perfect love is in you. And so you seek without for what you cannot find without."

T, 15, VI, 2:1-2

THE SPECIAL RELATIONSHIP IS AN ATTEMPT TO RE-ENACT THE PAST

"It is impossible to let the past go without relinquishing the special relationship. For the special relationship is an attempt to re-enact the past and change it. Imagined slights, remembered pain, past disappointments, perceived injustices and deprivations all enter into the special relationship, which becomes a way in which you seek to restore your wounded self-esteem."

T, 16, VII, 1:1-3

# Chapter 7

FAIRNESS: Am I Unfairly Treated?

Western Thinking
- I am unfairly treated.

Reverse Thinking
- I am responsible.

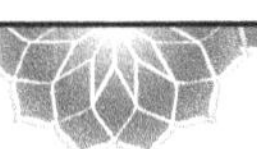

**Chapter 7 - Fairness:
Am I Unfairly Treated?**
Who doesn't think at one point, "Am I unfairly treated?" Reverse thinking opens the door to freedom from feelings of victimization. Watch this video to learn what *A Course in Miracles* teaches about feeling wronged or unfairly treated.

http://bit.ly/7Fairness

I AM RESPONSIBLE:
MY PERSONAL EXPERIENCE WITH THIS REVERSE THOUGHT

I was literally down on my hands and knees.

Please God, I prayed, *Please help me understand why I am in so much pain.*

I had recently attended a retreat with my boyfriend, during which I had discovered – in front of about sixty other people – that he had had multiple affairs throughout our relationship. This revelation left me with an unbelievable amount of emotional pain. Here is my story of betrayal, highlighting my belief in unfairness and my ultimate learning about love and responsibility.

LIAR, LIAR
When I learned of my partner's affairs during that personal growth workshop, the group's facilitator asked everyone assembled an amazing question.

He asked, "Who sides with whom on this issue?"

Then he asked my boyfriend and I to come and sit in the middle of the room facing each other, and he invited the other participants to go and sit behind the person (either me or my boyfriend) who they most sympathized with or related to in this situation.

I expected everyone to sit behind me. I truly wondered, *Who would ever sit behind the cheater?*
But to my great surprise, the room was evenly divided. Half of the people sat behind me and half sat behind my boyfriend. What a shock! And I was in for a few more.

When the room grew quiet, the facilitator looked at me and said, "It is obvious. You love a liar. How do you feel about that?"

"What? I do not feel good about that statement – not one little bit!" I answered.

"Well, it is the truth," he said, "and I am going to take this one step further and say I bet you have always loved liars!"

What? Was this man serious? I always loved liars? Even my boyfriend was outraged chiming in with, "No, I knew her past boyfriend, he is not a liar."

"Oh yes," the facilitator continued, "I am sure he is."

Could this situation get any more unreal? I thought. This facilitator didn't know my past boyfriend. How could he make such terrible accusations?

"Search your mind," he said, "I bet everyone you have ever loved has been a liar."

He continued, "I challenge you to think deeply when you go back to your room and your day-to-day world. Examine your past."

I left shocked, bewildered, and hurt. Had I truly always loved liars?

Later at home, still in pain that drove me to my knees, I noticed *A Course in Miracles* sitting on my shelf. The book had sat there for years, but I suddenly felt the need to look inside.

I closed my eyes and repeated my prayer, *Please God, please help me.* Then, I randomly opened the book. The first words I read said the following:

> *"Unfairness and attack are one mistake,*
> *so firmly joined that where one is perceived the other must be seen.*
> *You cannot be unfairly treated.*
> *The belief you are is but another form of the idea*
> *you are deprived by someone not yourself…*
> *You have no enemy except yourself."*
> T, 26, X, 3:1-6

What? My boyfriend had multiple affairs! Not one – many. I most certainly was unfairly treated. I was in disbelief. I read on.

> *"Beware of the temptation to perceive yourself unfairly treated.*
> *In this view, you seek to find an innocence that is not Theirs but yours alone,*
> *and at the cost of someone else's guilt.*
> *Can innocence be purchased by the giving of your guilt to someone else?"*
> T, 26, X, 4:1-3

I sat back. I couldn't believe it. I didn't believe it. However, something small and very quiet inside of me said very clearly to my soul, *This is the truth!*

I didn't like it. In fact, I hated what the book was saying to me, but something inside knew that my prayer had just been answered. I felt I was reading a truth, even if I didn't understand it. I knew this not in an intellectual way, but rather in a heartfelt way.

I did not understand what the quote had said, but I deeply wanted to. This inner motivation and curiosity led me to find an *A Course in Miracles* study group in my area. In this group, we spent the first hour reading the text and the second hour sharing miracles in our lives. At first, I felt totally confused by the text as I really did not understand it at all. Thankfully, the other participants were supportive. One member said, "Everyone feels that way at first – give it time." So, that is what I did. I gave it time. I kept on going to the group, and I kept on studying. I wanted to know the truth.

Eventually, what I discovered about myself truly amazed me: the group facilitator was right. When I started to look honestly at my past, I began to realize that I did love liars. The following is an account of how I arrived at this conclusion, which I had originally deeply denied.

My father was a brilliant architect, but he was also an alcoholic during my teen years, and he had lied all the time. After each and every drinking binge – and the resulting raw and wounded state my family would be left in – he would make a promise to never drink again. And for maybe six to eight months, he would keep his word. Inevitably, though, he would slide off the wagon and the binge drinking would return with a fury.

I used to think of him as Dr. Jekyll and Mr. Hyde. When he wasn't drinking, he was gentle, generous, teddy bear of a man. In fact, we called him "The Dancing Bear." When he was drinking though, he was verbally abusive and a terror to be around. I spent my teenage years being pushed to the forefront of the arguments between my mother and father. My mother hid behind me as I tried to get him to stop the verbal abuse, but it never worked. We prayed for him to pass out from the alcohol.

I had always excused my father in my own mind, because I loved him. He was my dad, and I wanted him to love me back. I did not want to turn his love away. However, when I examined my past, I could see that he lied about his drinking to us for years. He was the first liar I loved.

Okay, I got that connection, but what about my other boyfriends? Once again, I had to take very careful inventory, and what I learned surprised me.

Sure enough, just as the facilitator had predicted, every one of my boyfriends had lied to me in some way, shape, or form. For example, in one relationship, my boyfriend's parents were alcoholics and his family patterns were similar to mine. I wanted the two of us to examine these patterns together, but he refused to see the truth of his situation. He told me his family was fine, and that I was the one with the problem.

Well, he was right about that! It did seem like I was the one with a problem. Rather than get mad, I got curious.

- Why did I date guys that lied?
- What did I need to learn?

In order to answer these questions, I continued with my self-examination along with my study of *A Course in Miracles*, and I learned to ask the Holy Spirit for help. However, the answers did not come overnight. In fact, it took a couple of years of looking within and asking questions before I could clearly see the real root of the problem: I was the liar!

Surprised? I was to! After closely examining my life, I came to admit a hard truth: I did not lie to others, but I lied to myself all the time.

- I put up with behaviours that I did not like.
- I tried to get my boyfriends to change their evil ways.

Of course, neither of these strategies ever worked, although I couldn't see that at the time. It was the old case of "love is blind." I would make excuses for bad behaviour, and I would tell myself things would get better when they were obviously getting worse. Now, though, I could clearly see that I needed to take responsibility for lying to myself for years. With this discovery, I became clear and motivated. I realized, deeply and fully, that I was the one who needed to change – not my boyfriends.

There was no book that said these men needed to change, and for good reason. Heck, I had long ago learned (after many counselling sessions) that if my father wanted to drink himself to death, it was not my job to save him. He had to take responsibility for his own life; I could not take on that responsibility for him.

This process of self-discovery around the topic of lying resulted in a 180-degree turn around in my perception. No one was unfairly treating me, I was unfairly treating myself. I was depriving myself. I was putting up with things I did not like or want in my life. I needed to clearly say that these men did not need to change – instead, I needed to change my thinking and get aligned with love rather than fear.

Years later, I can see that I was thinking with my wrong mind. I was afraid of losing love, so I lied to myself about what I could and could not tolerate. The men I dated were simply showing up as mirrors for what was going on within myself. I needed to start thinking that the love was not outside of myself, but inside.

This was a profound and deep turn around in thinking.
I could see there was no enemy.
I was not a victim.

I was trying to teach myself, with every relationship, about the nature of true love.
Love does not exist outside myself.
Love lives within. I cannot lose it.
Love cannot run away or reject me.
How would that be love? It is contrary to the very nature of love.
Love is eternal.
I knew that instinctively – in my gut, in my intuition – and had now grown to know that consciously.

I eventually chose to leave the relationship with the man who had many affairs. However, I chose not to leave mad, but rather with love in my heart for all the life learning I had done with him. I chose to be responsible for myself and for my feelings, and to stay aligned with the love within.

Today, I feel a deep and special gratitude for every man who I dated. They were, in fact, my most precious teachers. I often fantasize that when this physical body dies, before I leave the physical realm, I will be able to visit each one in spirit and thank them for being among my greatest teachers.

In the end, I learned I cannot be unfairly treated. I am responsible for what I see and how I see it. By changing my mind, and changing my perception, I turned my story of being a victim into being a victor.

Every relationship is indeed a lesson in love.

WHAT DOES *A COURSE IN MIRACLES* SAY ABOUT FAIRNESS?

I hate to admit it, but being unfairly treated has been one of my central life lessons. In the previous story, the lesson was truly right in my face: I attracted a liar into my life because I was lying to myself. Relationships are outer mirrors of what is going on inside our minds. As my teacher had pointed out to me, I had learned to love liars and excuse their behaviour. I was projecting what I had learned out onto my world and attracting the same thing over and over.

It was not easy to pull back the painful curtains of blame and attack. In fact, the world supported the idea that in this situation, I was the victim. However, playing the victim is aligning with the ego – an attack on one's self. Rather than believing the best about myself – that I am whole and complete – I believed I was deprived and scarce. This victim position never makes us happy, instead it robs us of our joy and freedom by tying us to the past. Here is a great quote from the course about this concept:

"The past is gone;
seek not to preserve it in the special relationship that binds you to it,
and would teach you salvation is past
and so you must return to the past to find salvation.
There is no fantasy that does not contain the dream of retribution for the past.
Would you act out the dream or let it go?"
T, 16, VII, 4:1-3

I love the end question: *"Would you act out the dream or let it go?"* The dream is the story I tell myself over and over again about being unfairly treated. In order not to repeat this behaviour, I must stop trying to change other people's behaviour. Instead, I have to look clearly at changing my own mind about what is going on. I am not being unfairly treated – I am projecting a belief I have onto the world, and it is manifesting in front of me. To release myself from this type of behaviour, I needed to ask the Holy Spirit for assistance in changing my mind. I have learned by studying *A Course in Miracles* that when I give the reins of control over to the one who has my highest interest in mind, miracles happen – miracles that I could not even begin to imagine.

"The Holy Spirit can use all that you give to Him for your salvation.
But He cannot use what you withhold,
for He cannot take it from you without your willingness."
T, 25, VIII, 1:1-2

"No one deserves to lose. And what would be unjust to him cannot occur.
Healing must be for everyone, because he does not merit an attack of any kind.
What order can there be in miracles,
unless someone deserves to suffer more and others less?
And is this justice to the wholly innocent?
A miracle is justice.
It is not a special gift to some, to be withheld from others as less worthy,
more condemned, and thus apart from healing.
Who is there who can separate from salvation, if its purpose is the end of specialness."

T, 25, IX, 6:1-8

UNFAIRNESS AND ATTACK ARE ONE MISTAKE

"Unfairness and attack are one mistake, so firmly joined that where one is perceived the other must be seen. You cannot be unfairly treated. The belief you are is but another form of the idea you are deprived by someone not yourself.

T, 26, X, 3:1-3

YOU HAVE NO ENEMY EXCEPT YOURSELF

"You have no enemy except yourself."

T, 26, X, 3:6

BEWARE THE TEMPTATION TO PERCEIVE YOURSELF UNFAIRLY TREATED

"Beware of the temptation to perceive yourself unfairly treated. In this view, you seek to find an innocence that is not Theirs but yours alone, and at the cost of someone else's guilt. Can innocence be purchased by the giving of your guilt to someone else?"

T, 26, X, 4:1-3

THE RESPONSIBILITY FOR SIGHT

"I am responsible for what I see.
I choose the feelings I experience,
and I decide upon the goal I would achieve.
And everything that seems to happen to me
I ask for, and receive as I have asked.
Deceive yourself no longer that you are helpless in the face of what is done to you.
Acknowledge but that you have been mistaken, all effects of your mistakes will disappear."

T, 21, II, 2:3-7

YOU HAVE THE RIGHT TO PERFECT PEACE

"You have the right to all the universe; to perfect peace, complete deliverance from all effects of sin, and to the life eternal, joyous and complete in every way, as God appointed for His holy son."

T, 25, VIII, 14:1

GOD'S LAWS ARE ALWAYS FAIR

"God's laws are always fair and perfectly consistent. By giving you receive. But to receive is to accept, not to get. It is impossible not to have, but it is possible not to know you have. The recognition of having is the willingness for giving, and only by this willingness can you recognize what you have."

T, 9, II, 11:3-7

WHEN A BROTHER BEHAVES INSANELY

"When a brother behaves insanely, you can heal him only by perceiving the sanity in him. If you perceive his errors and accept them, you are accepting yours. If you want to give yours over to the Holy Spirit, you must do this with his. Unless this becomes the one way in which you handle all errors, you cannot understand how all errors are undone."

T, 9, III, 5:1-4

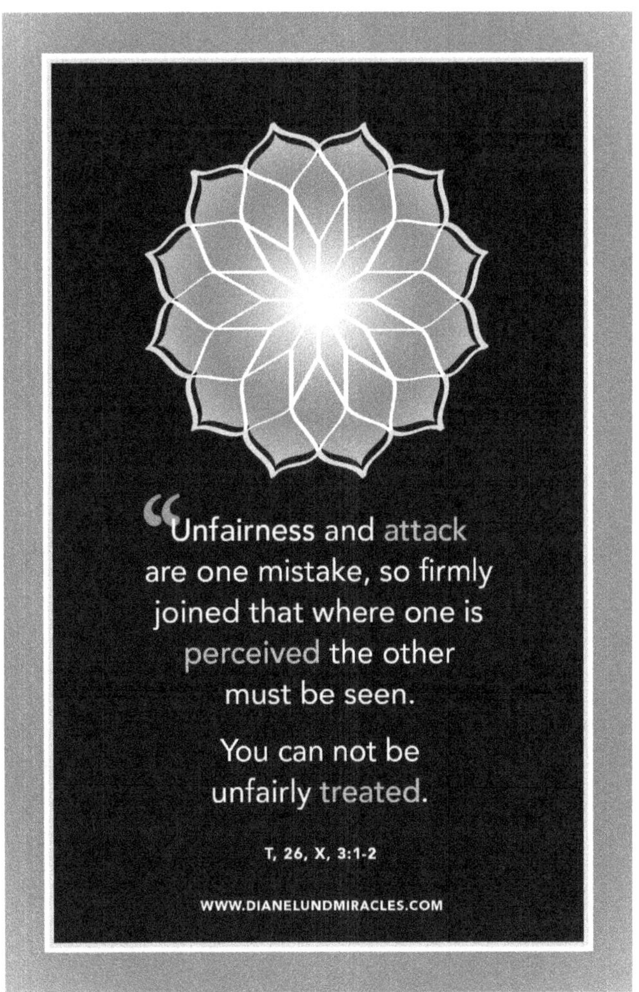

# Chapter 8

ALONE: Are We Alone?

Western Thinking
- We are alone.

Reverse Thinking
- We are never alone.

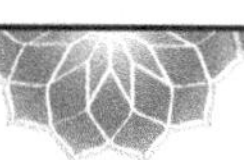

Chapter 8 - Alone: Are We Alone?
When I was young, I was afraid of being alone. Now, I never feel alone. Watch this video to find out how I transformed from lonely and constantly searching to feeling complete and whole, just as I am.

http://bit.ly/8Alone

WE ARE NEVER ALONE:
MY PERSONAL EXPERIENCE WITH THIS REVERSE THOUGHT

As a child, I always felt alone. I made up a story that I came from another planet, and that I had landed in the wrong family. No one seemed to understand me.

My mom was baffled and bothered by my questions.

"Go away," she said, "You ask too many questions. I don't know the answers. Leave me alone." Or when things got bad, she would lock herself in her bedroom and cry, "Just go away. Stop bugging me!"

The kind of questions I was prone to asking, and that perturbed my mother, were vast and far-reaching.
- How many stars exist?
- Where do we come from?
- What is God?
- How do I talk to him?
- Why don't we go to church?
- Why do some people suffer and others do not?

There was just no end to what I wanted to know, and this steady stream of unending questions frightened my mom.

My dad tried to answer these questions the best he could, but he did not believe in a God or a higher power. He believed we come from dust, and we return to dust. That just seemed way too simple, and consequently, untrue – at least in my mind.

Look around, I thought, *This whole universe has come from somewhere. There must be something more – something that thought it all up or conceived of it in order for it to manifest.*

Dad's answer was, "The world evolved from gases and molecules coming together." I did not doubt this was true on some level, I just felt it was not the whole story. I longed for something that really seemed to resonate with my own inner feelings. My dad's answers just left me cold and searching for more.

Needless to say, I felt alone – a feeling that persisted in my life for many, many years. I didn't want to be alone, so I searched for relationships that would comfort me and not leave me abandoned in the end. This is another chapter in my story, but the search for the perfect relationship never worked either (although I must say I gave it a valiant try). The fact of the matter is, we all feel alone at times, whether it is physically alone, mentally alone, spiritually alone, or emotionally alone. It is a common human experience.

PHYSICALLY ALONE

We have all experienced times when we were the only body in a room. We were alone – at least, that is what our physical eyes and ears told us. There was no one there to hold our hand or assure us that things would work out just fine. We thought we were alone because we believed our physical senses.

So, why does *A Course in Miracles* say we are never alone? Because it is not referring to the reality of you as a human body, but rather the reality of you as an eternal spirit. *A Course in Miracles* takes the perspective that we are all one, joined through one spirit and one mind. When we turn our focus from the outside world to our internal world, we can access this connection to all. It is something we have all heard about. We are one.

A Course in Miracles points out that it is important to understand that the human mind is split into two. The part of the mind that thinks it is separated from the eternal and alone is called the ego mind, or the wrong mind, while the part of the mind that knows it can never be separated from eternal love is called the Holy Spirit or the right mind. The course says we constantly switch back and forth between these perspectives, and that where we put our focus determines how we think and what we perceive. When we look around the room and see that we are physically alone, we can choose to feel alone and lonely and believe our physical senses. Or we can sit back in our chair, close our eyes, and connect with our inner spirit. In this place, we are connected to all that is – to God. When we feel this profound connection, we know we are not alone and never need to be alone again.

After years and years of practice, I can happily say I rarely feel alone anymore. Through my spiritual pursuits, I have found the small, still voice within that communicates with me on an ongoing basis.

THE SMALL, STILL VOICE WITHIN

By now you might be asking, how do I find this inner connection – this small voice within? Well, one thing is certain: you can't just call your inner voice on your cell phone. First, I think it important to acknowledge that we all hear this voice from time to time. For example, imagine you are asked to go to a party. Inside, one voice tells you that it is not a good idea to go – you are exhausted and need time to yourself. But then another voice, your ego voice, demands, *I don't want to miss tonight's party. I might miss meeting someone special.*

In the end, you go to the party out of fear of missing out – the inner voice is overruled by the ego voice. But once the party is over, you think, *That party was a waste of time. My gut feeling telling me not to go was right! Why didn't I listen to my inner voice?* You heard your inner voice, but you didn't want to believe it because you were fearful of missing out. Consequently, you denied what you knew at a deeper level, although you did not want to consciously acknowledge that fact. In situations like this, it can seem like our inner voice is hidden from us. In reality, though, it is often just below our conscious awareness.

WHY DON'T WE LISTEN TO OUR INNER VOICE?

The reason we don't listen to our inner voice is because we think we know better. Internally, whether you are aware of it or not, you are always choosing what voice you listen to. Some people say that the ego speaks loudest and first, and this is often true. In the case of going to the party, the voice that wants you to take care of yourself is overruled by the voice that does not want to miss out. If you think about this situation carefully, one voice is coming from fear. It says, *I don't want to miss anything.* Behind this voice is a belief in lack – a belief that you don't have enough. The other voice, the one that says, *Be kind to yourself and rest,* comes from a loving perspective.

Searching for something in the physical world may deliver satisfaction for a time. Unfortunately, that time always ends. People change, and circumstances change. When we feel alone, we are really feeling our separation from God – from the part of ourselves that is connected with everything.

We can spend ages searching the outside world for something to take away the ache, but the answer to the real problem is always found within.

MY TRUE LOVE STORY

This truth is one that I have become personally familiar with because I spent years looking for true love on the outside. I believed that if I could just find the right person, then surely my life would be better. But try as hard as I might, it just wasn't happening. I dated and dated and dated. I had my list – my ideas of what I thought would work in a relationship. But the older I got, the more exhausted and unhappy I became with the dating game. Finally, I decided I'd had enough. I put away my list, got down on my hands and knees, and once again prayed.

I said to the Holy Spirit (the voice for God that lives within us), *Obviously, I am not a good judge of who I should be with. So, I now place this situation and my list of who I think I should be with not in my hands, but in yours. I declared, I will stop judging. I will stop looking at my list, and I will be open to anyone you bring into my life.*

I put my list of what I wanted behind a picture in a frame so that whenever I looked at that photo, I would remember that I had made a commitment to myself that I would let the Holy Spirit take control of my relationships. In essence, I gave the control of my relationships over to God. I told myself, *I will align with God and not my own limited desires.*

Guess what happened? The person who next asked me out was absolutely nothing like my list.
- I wanted someone who had never been married; this man was previously married.
- I wanted a man who was tall; this man was short.

- I wanted a man who had no kids; this man had two.
- I wanted a man who was spiritual; this man had left the Catholic religion behind, and he was bitter about the whole experience.
- I wanted a man with hair; this man was bald.
- I wanted someone gentle; this man had been in the army and barked out orders.

As you may have guessed, this man, this not-on-my-list man, turned out to be the man I would marry.

To this day, I believe God picked my husband for me – I truly did not pick him – and the only reason I was open to dating him was because I had put away the list of my own desires and turned my face and heart to God. I stopped judging what I thought I wanted and opened myself to what God delivered.

WHAT HELPED ME DO THIS.

I knew from direct experience that no one could make me happy – I was the only person who could fill that job opening. And when I stepped into loving myself and connecting with my own spirit as I searched for the answers to being alone, I learned I was never alone.

My past experience had taught me God is always there, waiting for me. As a matter of fact, the man I married had been right there all along. I had known him on a casual basis for many years, I just never considered dating him.

Now that I knew I was never alone, I was free to open up my mind to new possibilities. I did not need a partner to be anything other than his authentic self. I did not need a partner to cure or end my loneliness or my unhappiness. I did not need a partner to be by my side at all times. I had discovered that God is always with me, and that I was the eternal love I was looking for.

I could be with someone on the outside without needing that person because I was happy on the inside. Funny how that works! I had proved to myself, once again, that choosing to connect with something that is unseen and invisible to the eye is life-altering.

WHAT DOES *A COURSE IN MIRACLES* SAY ABOUT BEING ALONE?

Right up there with being unfairly treated, being alone has always been a big concern in my life. When I was younger, I was afraid of being alone. In fact, I often felt alone in a room full of people because there were not many people who wanted to talk to me in depth about the questions that were renting space in my mind.

A counsellor once asked me, "What are you really afraid of?"

I said, "I am afraid of being alone."

He got a puzzled look on his face, then said, "From everything you have told me, it looks like you have almost always been alone."

Wow, I thought, *I have never thought of it like that.* And you know, he was right.

For most of my life, I was alone in what I was seeking. There was no support from my family unless I worked for it – they were just too wrapped up in their own problems. In my mother and father's eyes, I was strong and therefore did not need their attention or support. They believed I could handle things myself, and that opinion was both a blessing and a curse. It helped me to be strong, but it often left me feeling alone.

What a joy it was for me to finally discover that I am never alone. Personally, I found this treasure by looking within – by believing my inner guide and not relying on my outer circumstances. As I practised listening to my inner voice and turning my troubles over to the Holy Spirit, I experienced a connectedness I could not deny. I learned I just needed to ask. I am never alone because the inner voice for love and for God, which *A Course in Miracles* calls the Holy Spirit, is always with me. It will lead me with inner prompts and messages. If I do not hear anything within, there is probably nothing else to know in this moment. My inner guide never lets me down.

YOU CANNOT REMEMBER GOD IN SECRET AND ALONE
"It is impossible to remember God in secret and alone. For remembering Him means you are not alone, and are willing to remember it."
T, 14, X, 10:1-1

THE LONELY JOURNEY FAILS

"The lonely journey fails because it has excluded what it would find."

T, 14, X, 10:7

YOU CANNOT BE ALONE AS "I AM ALWAYS WITH YOU"

"When I said, 'I am with you always,' I meant it literally. I am not absent to anyone in any situation. Because I am always with you, you are the way, the truth and the life. You did not make this power any more than I did. It was created to be shared, and therefore cannot be meaningfully perceived as belonging to anyone at the expense of another."

T, 7, III, 1:7-11

ALONE WE ARE ALL LOWLY, BUT TOGETHER WE SHINE WITH BRIGHTNESS

"Alone we are all lowly, but together we shine with brightness so intense that none of us alone can even think of it."

T, 13, X, 14:2

AN ILLUSION OF ISOLATION

"I come as a light into a world that does deny itself everything. It does this simply by dissociating itself from everything. It is therefore an illusion of isolation, maintained by fear of the same loneliness that is its illusion. I said that I am with you always, even unto the end of the world. That is why I am the light of the world. If I am with you in the loneliness of the world, the loneliness is gone. You cannot maintain the illusion of loneliness as you are not alone."

T, 8, IV, 2:1-7

THE EGO IS THE PART OF THE MIND

"The ego is the part of the mind that believes your existence is defined by separation."

T, 4, VII, 1:5

SEEK NOT OUTSIDE YOURSELF

"Seek not outside yourself. For it will fail, and you will weep each time an idol falls. Heaven cannot be found where it is not, and there can be no peace excepting (sic) there. Each idol that you worship when God calls will never answer in His place. There is no other answer you can substitute, and find the happiness His answer brings. Seek not outside yourself."

T, 29, VII, 1:1-6

 # Chapter 9

GRIEVANCES: Whose Fault Is It?

Western Thinking
- My grievances are someone else's fault.

Reverse Thinking
- My grievances are my responsibility.

Chapter 9 - Grievance: Whose Fault Is It? Do you find yourself blaming people or circumstances? Watch this video to find out why, according to *A Course in Miracles*, holding grievances just holds back your quality of life, and what you can do about it.

http://bit.ly/9Grievance

MY GRIEVANCES ARE MY RESPONSIBILITY:
MY PERSONAL EXPERIENCE WITH THIS REVERSE THOUGHT

Attending residential self-development programs at a centre called The Haven on Gabriola Island, British Columbia, Canada, was one of the great experiences of my life. I first went to a couple's workshop to get help for my distressing relationships, but one workshop, like one potato chip, just wasn't enough to satisfy my craving. I wanted to understand myself better, so I started to take their personal growth courses and workshops.

The second one I took was called Come Alive, without a doubt it was true to its name. Everyone in that workshop came alive through the exercises, discussions, and bodywork we did over the course of five days.

If you wanted to go even more in depth, you could take their month-long programs called Phases. Phase One addressed **The Self** while Phase Two addressed **The Self and Others**. I wanted to understand myself better, so I was committed to going to these programs.

Every day, we went to class from 9:00 a.m. to noon. We then had a lunch break until 3:00 p.m., at which point we would return to the self-growth work. After a dinner break, we broke into small groups from 7:00 p.m. to 9:00 p.m. Each phase gave us a chance to look deep within using bodywork, Gestalt, visualization, drama, and even Chinese acupuncture. I was terrified and captivated all at the same time.

In one particular course, our leader said we were going to have a competition entitled, "Who Is the Biggest Victim?" We were told to think about everything that had gone wrong in our lives and pick a story where we felt like a victim. Then, during the three-hour morning session, each participant would go to the front of the room and share their personal victim story.

I thought to myself, *Wow! I have a bevy of bad experiences to choose from – I mean, who doesn't?* However, one incident truly stood out in my mind.

THE BIGGEST VICTIM

When I was about seventeen, both sets of my grandparents lived a ferry ride away on Vancouver Island. One day, we first went to visit my dad's family in Sydney and then drove to Nanaimo to my mother's mom's funeral. My dad was still in his bad drinking phase and had begun drinking with his family before we left, so the ride up the island highway was not fun. It was a dark and stormy night as the saying goes, both inside and outside our car.

My mom was extremely unhappy that my dad was driving the car after drinking, but my dad was overconfident and told her, "I am just fine." We all knew this wasn't true, but we prayed we would get to my grandparents' house. We had been in this position with my father many times before, and we knew he would stubbornly cling to his assertion that he was "just fine," even if he was drunk.

The next day was my grandmother Lily's funeral, and the day went from bad to worse. Dad continued with his binge drinking and made a big scene at the funeral, saying awful things about my grandma because she had never approved of my dad marrying my mom. He was bitter, and – with a few drinks in him – the sour words that were flooding out of his mouth stunned the other guests.

My mom was both heartsick and mortified. She just wanted to get rid of him, so she told him to go home and take us with him. I was shocked. I did not want to go home with my dad – he was drunk, and I was scared to be with him. My siblings felt the same. We told her we did not want to go, but she insisted. She needed time alone with her family. So, my sisters and I got in the car with my dad and got in the lineup for the ferry to cross back over the water to our home in Vancouver.

We were all extremely frightened of my dad when he had been drinking – he was mean and unkind in what he said. We knew better than to argue or say something that might set him off.

When we disembarked the ferry in our car, my father – still in his savage mood – told us he was going to kill us all by driving off the steep cliff adjacent to the highway near our home. My sisters and I were terrified. I pleaded with him, but he kept swerving off the highway onto the gravel and then swerving back onto the road. My sisters were now crying in the back seat, and I was screaming at him to stop playing around. We were truly scared. He was so out of control that I honestly thought we were going to die.

To make matters worse, I was old enough to be able to get a driver's license, so I felt I should be able to take over and drive the car. However, I didn't have my license yet. I was wracked with guilt about not being able to protect my two sisters. What could I do?

I decided to roll down the window and shout to passing cars to save us. I hung out the window and waved at the other vehicles.

"Help! My dad is trying to kill us! Help us please!" I screamed.

Soon, the people in their cars started to notice, and they began to follow us. This made my dad angrier. He started swerving more, repeatedly heading for the cliff and then turning back onto the road.

My heart was beating out of my chest. My sisters were crying and screaming with me in the back seat. Dad drove faster and faster. We could not get him to stop.

"PULL OVER AND STOP THE CAR!" I screamed with all my might.

Finally, he took the nearest exit and headed for a side street. The minute the car stopped, I leapt out as fast as I could and ran to the nearest house. I banged on the door and told the people who answered that I needed to use their phone to call the police because my dad was trying to kill us. They were horrified, of course, and they let me in to make the call.

I told the police what had happened and where we were, and they immediately came to arrest my father, and take us home. We spent the night by ourselves, frightened out of our minds. What had we done to deserve such awful treatment from our parents?

After this event, I was shaking with grief over my grandma's death and the cruelty and insensitivity of my father, who thought the whole thing was just one big joke. I thought it was insanity. I was a mess of feelings – grief, guilt, outrage, and terror – and I was feeling them all at once! In my mind, I truly believed I was the biggest victim.

Once everyone had told their tale of woe, our leaders told us to vote for the person with the worst victim story – and I won! Everyone agreed that my story had been the worst. However, that is not where this story ends. One of the leaders announced that during our lunch break, we were to think how our stories could be told in a different way.

He said, "Think of how your story could be told in such a way that each of us were one hundred percent responsible for everything that had happened."

What? I thought. *They must be crazy! How could that terrifying event be my fault? How was I responsible for my dad's insane behaviour?* I was absolutely at a loss.

HOW WAS I RESPONSIBLE FOR THIS TERRIFYING EVENT?
I wracked my brain for possible answers as I ate my lunch that day, and then later as I walked along the beach. It took me hours of deep, deep thinking and questioning before it occurred to me that another person might have acted differently. Slowly, I saw that I had been making decisions at every step, and another person might have made very different decisions. I was the person who decided how to see the event and how to act within it. This realization was like a light bulb going on.

For example, what if I had stood up to my mom and refused to get in the car with my dad? What if I had realized how drunk my dad was on the ferry, refused to get back in the car, and just walked off with my sisters and called a cab instead?

My mind started to spin out alternative scenarios. I started to see that many factors went into how I played the game of life that day. I saw how I did not want to upset my mom further because she was struggling with the grief of her mom's passing. I knew she wanted me to go with my dad because she thought I could handle him better than she could, and I didn't want to disappoint her. I wanted to protect my younger sisters, and I felt the need to play the role my family had given me.

Suddenly, I saw clearly that other people might have had different motivations and reacted differently. I also began to see that my decisions and motivations helped to create the situation that had occurred.

The funny thing is that the more I started to take ownership of the situation in my mind, the better I felt. Instead of feeling worse about the whole ugly event, I started to feel my own power. In time, I realized my power rested in how I thought about the situation and why I made those decisions that day. I understood that different people might have behaved differently, and that I behaved the way I did because of the choices I made.

In our small groups that evening, we all had an opportunity to tell our new stories and discuss why we were responsible for what happened in our lives. It was illuminating and heart opening to hear how everyone turned his or her story around. Instead of being victims, we now saw that we could be the heroes and heroines of our own lives simply by understanding that we are always in control of what we decide and what we think. This was the beginning of my decision to be responsible for what I saw in every situation. I could see that holding on to grievances equated to holding on to victimhood, and that state left me powerless. Taking responsibility for how I saw the situations in my life was the road to freedom.

I keep walking that road today.

WHAT DOES *A COURSE IN MIRACLES* SAY ABOUT GRIEVANCES?

It is difficult to hold grievances – it is like holding your hand in a fist and refusing to let go. It takes way more energy to hold a fist than it does to open up and release the tension.

Grievances are like swallowing poison and hoping the other person dies. They put us in a permanent state of dis-ease, and this state blocks our awareness of love. It says love cannot come in, that love is off limits, and in this way we prove ourselves right. Love does not win out when we believe we are victims. Often, we hold to this victim position because we think it will make others feel sorry for us, and because it makes us feel we do not have to do anything. We can be self-righteous, believing there is nothing for us to change.

The thought of changing our minds is really what frightens us. We want to be right even if it hurts us, tires us, and defeats us. We believe our evaluation of our story, and we want everyone else to come in line with our position. There is a famous quote from the course that says,

> *"Do you prefer that you be right or happy?"*
>
> T, 29, VII, 1:9

What we want is for the other person to be wrong. We desperately want to believe that if the world and the people in it would just get in line, there would be no problem. We want to order things outside of ourselves rather than reordering our own thinking. We are deeply invested in our own position. We do not want to change; we want the world around us to change. Believing that something outside of ourselves can bring us happiness is our great white hope – the thing our ego clings to. The idea of giving up our investment is unthinkable to the ego; it wants to be right, even if we suffer. In fact, suffering just proves to the ego that we are right. How twisted is this concept? And yet we all do it. We all cling to ideas that hurt.

The way out is to reverse our thinking. Instead of holding grievances, we must look at our responsibility in their existence.

THE EGO'S PLAN FOR SALVATION CENTERS AROUND HOLDING GRIEVANCES

"The ego's plan for salvation centers around holding grievances. It maintains that, if someone else spoke or acted differently, if some external circumstance or event were changed, you would be saved. Thus, the source of salvation is constantly perceived as outside yourself. Each grievance you hold is a declaration, and an assertion in which you believe, that says, 'If this were different, I would be saved'."

W, L71, 2:1-4

MY GRIEVANCES HIDE THE LIGHT OF THE WORLD IN ME

"No one can look upon what your grievances conceal. Because your grievances are hiding the light of the world in you, everyone stands in darkness, and you beside him. But as the veil of your grievances is lifted, you are released with him."

W, L69, 1:1-2

YOUR PICTURE OF THE WORLD MIRRORS WHAT IS WITHIN

"Your picture of the world can only mirror what is within. The source of neither light nor darkness can be found without. Grievances darken your mind, and you look out of a darkened world. Forgiveness lifts the darkness, reasserts our will, and lets you look upon a world of light."

W, L73, 5:1-4

LET MIRACLES REPLACE ALL GRIEVANCES

"Perhaps it is not yet quite clear to you that each decision that you make is one between a grievance and a miracle. Each grievance stands like a dark shield against the miracle it would conceal."

W, L78, 1:1-2

THE WAY OUT OF CONFLICT

"The way out of conflict between two opposing thought systems is clearly to choose one and relinquish the other."

T, 6, B, 5:1

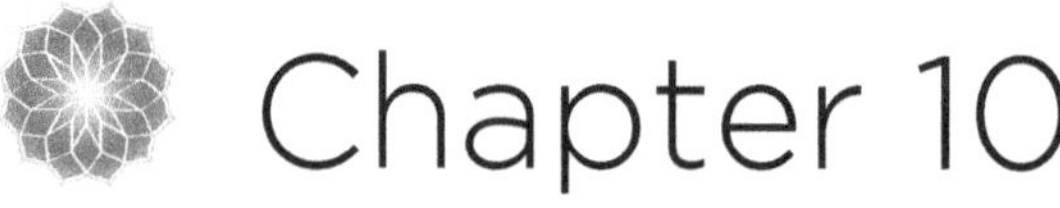# Chapter 10

CORRECTION: Who Do You Need to Change?

Western Thinking

- I need people to change.

Reverse Thinking

- I need myself to change.

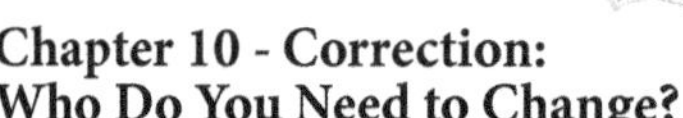

Chapter 10 - Correction: Who Do You Need to Change?
Do you believe your life would be happier if only person "x" or loved-one "y" could change in certain ways? Then this lesson is for you. Watch this video to learn what *A Course in Miracles* says about correcting or trying to change others.

http://bit.ly/10Correction

I NEED MYSELF TO CHANGE:
MY PERSONAL EXPERIENCE WITH THIS REVERSE THOUGHT

Wanting or needing to correct or change people is a commonly sung refrain of the human condition.

Consider how many times in your life you have thought the following:
If only I could get
- *my boyfriend to change,*
- *my kids to change,*
- *my mother-in-law to change, or*
- *my boss to change,*

then my world would certainly be a better place.

This type of thinking really wastes time and usually gets under other people's skin. The truth is that most people do not want to change. They like how they do things, and they don't want to get any flack about it. We usually just make people angry and frustrated when we want them to change, because the underlying message is, *You are doing it wrong.* And people generally want to be right, not wrong. So, they fight, or withdraw, or avoid, or complain, or rebel, but they do not change. Instead, they often dig their heels in and the situation becomes worse. So, what can we do? Well, here is a story from my own life to illustrate how I had a total reversal in thinking.

THE STORY OF THE LIGHTHOUSE

I went to see a coach because I was working too much, and she had a process she said would turn my behaviour around. She said it would take about four sessions, each one about three hours long.

On the third session, she had me do a long internal visualization. She took me through many steps, and after an hour and a half I saw the following vision.

In my inner sight, I was a lighthouse with a big light rotating around and around, casting its light out onto the water. In my visualization, I heard a voice that said, *Look out on the water and see all the boats.* I cast my gaze out on the water and indeed, I did see many boats moving in different directions.

An internal voice spoke to me and said, *You want to help the people in their different boats get to their destination with your light, but look closely and see how the people are reacting.*
- *Some people are rowing away from the light.*
- *Some people are rowing towards the light.*
- *Some people are just going their own way.*

- *Others are sitting in their boats mending nets.*
- *Still others are jumping overboard.*
- *Some people are arguing in their boat.*
- *Some people are kissing.*

You want to tell the people in the boat what to do.
- *Row faster.*
- *Row in the other direction.*
- *Pay attention to the rocks.*

And still other times, you want to jump in their boat and help them row ashore. This behaviour is not helpful. People need to be the captain of their own craft. You really have just one job and one job only. And that job is to:

BLINK, BLINK, BLINK.

And in case you didn't get it, I will repeat. All you need to do is:

BLINK, BLINK, BLINK.

I started to laugh out loud. I knew exactly what the internal voice was telling me to do – it was telling me to stop trying to adjust other people's behaviour.

The voice continued, *The best thing you can do is do what you do best. Send out your light.*

BLINK, BLINK, BLINK.

The answer seemed so simple. The voice resumed, *Stop trying to tell people what to do or how to do it, and certainly stop jumping into other people's boats to try to help them row. All of this is interfering, and when you are interfering with their lives you are not doing your job. And your job is one thing, and one thing only:*

BLINK, BLINK, BLINK.

When I opened my eyes to talk with the coach about what I had just experienced, she asked me why I was laughing so hard. I told her what I had seen within my visualization.

I said I had a girlfriend who had died in her forties who used to have a company called Lighthouse. I knew when I saw myself as a lighthouse that she had something to do with the visualization. Then, I heard a voice telling me that I needed to stop interfering with other people's boats and just share my light. I needed to do one job and one job only, and that was to:

BLINK, BLINK, BLINK.

"Funny thing," I told her, "It was my girlfriend's voice that I heard in my head during the visualization; the one who died. It was her voice giving me the instructions."

Then I heard myself saying, "I would like to test something out. I would like to test the universe."

"Test the universe?" my coach said, puzzled. "I have never heard of such a thing!" I told her, "I want to know if the voice I heard in my head was the voice of my girlfriend." I told her this was nothing new for me – I often asked the universe for help and assistance.

"Okay, what do you want to do?" she asked.

I told her, "My girlfriend's husband has not been in touch with me since she died. If the voice is the voice of my friend, I ask the universe to get her husband to contact me within a week."

"I don't care how he does it. I just want to hear from her husband as confirmation that it was indeed my good friend helping me with my visualization and understanding."

So, I asked the universe. And guess what? Within a couple of days, her husband emailed me for the first time in years! It felt like a miracle, and like a confirmation of what I knew in my heart to be true: my girlfriend was helping and guiding me from the other side. Plus, it was proof to me that we have a dynamic and responsive relationship with the universe. As it is often said, "Ask and you shall receive."

I have never forgotten the simple message of that inner vision. My job was one thing and one thing only: to shine my light.

BLINK, BLINK, BLINK.

In addition, the visualization clearly told me to stop trying to change or help people with their jobs.
- Do your job.
- Do not try and change other people.
- Change yourself instead.

I can tell you today, years after having this vision, that this simple advice still works.

WHAT DOES *A COURSE IN MIRACLES* SAY ABOUT CHANGING OTHERS?

A Course in Miracles says most people think they are right because they are the ones making up their own mind. They are the ones who are literally making up their reality, and just like God loves what he creates so do we love what we make.

A Course in Miracles also says God creates by extending love, and that we make our worlds appear in a similar way. However, instead of extending love, we project our thoughts outwards. Our thoughts can have their origin in love or fear because we live with a separated mind: one side is the ego mind or wrong mind, and the other side is the Holy Spirit, also known as right mind.

Projected fearful thoughts (ego thoughts) have power, just like projected loving thoughts. These thoughts go out into the world and powerfully magnetize electrons to create our physical world, according to quantum physics.

The course says fearful thoughts are mis-creations, and I think we often see these mis-creations as mis-takes. I like the idea of missed-takes instead because I have worked as a broadcast producer for many years. In the film business, when a director is shooting a scene he calls for "take one," followed by "take two." Similarly, when we mis-create by thinking with our ego or our fear, *A Course in Miracles* says we can simply choose another thought.

Here's what I think of when I make a mis-take: *Hey, that was just take one, and I need a redo. Let's try another way of thinking. How can I change this situation by thinking not from fear, but from love? Instead of believing I need to correct others, perhaps I need to correct my own thinking.*

The course says correction of others is never our function. We are rarely conscious when we are thinking from fear, guilt, and pain, but our feelings let us know what is truly happening. If we feel sad, frustrated, angry, or hurt, we must be thinking from fear. God, or our source, never detours from love. When we turn correction over to the Holy Spirit, which is the voice for God and for love, we free ourselves. We need to let go of playing God.

The course calls this The Authority Problem. We are not the authority on the universe, even if we want to think we are. We do not know what is best for other people – what they should or should not do. When we think we know what is best for others, we play God. We literally say to the universe, "My opinion and judgment are more important than God's." *A Course in Miracles* calls this true arrogance.

CORRECTION IS NOT YOUR FUNCTION

"Correction is not your function. It belongs to One Who knows of fairness, not of guilt. If you assume correction's role, you lose the function of forgiveness."

T, 27, II, 10:1-3

LEAVE CORRECTION TO THE ONE: THE HOLY SPIRIT

"Correction must be left to One Who knows correction and forgiveness are the same. With half a mind, this is not understood. Leave, then, correction to the Mind that is united, functioning as one because it is not split in purpose, and conceives a single function as its only one."

T, 27, II, 16:1-3

CORRECTION IS OF GOD

"Any attempt you make to correct a brother means that you believe correction by you is possible, and this can only be the arrogance of the ego. Correction is of God, Who does not know of arrogance."

T, 9, III, 7:8-9

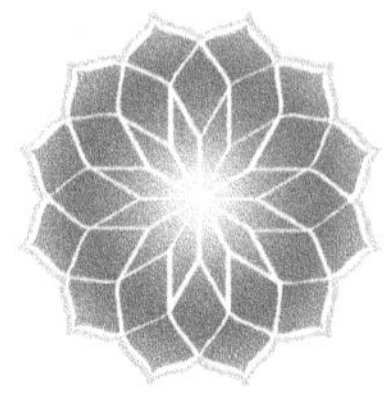

PART THREE

WORK AND MONEY:
How Do You Define Success?

*"The value of a man
should be seen in what he gives
and not in what he is able to receive."*
Albert Einstein

INTRODUCTION

HARD WORK

I was born into a family that believed in hard work. My father was the first of his family to go to university and get a degree, and he paid a high price for it. His father was a fisherman, and he wanted my dad to go fishing with him and help on the boats. When my dad decided to go to university instead and get a higher education, my grandfather disowned him and refused to talk to him. True to his own heart, my dad defied his father and followed his own path, regardless of the consequences. My grandmother loved them both and got stuck in between the two of them. She even had to sneak out to see her son during that period. My dad struggled to work and pay for his schooling because his family refused to help him. Consequently, my dad treasured his education and wanted all three of his daughters to go to university. He considered it a privilege to receive a higher education and taught us that you have to work hard for what you want. In addition, he taught us that the universe does not hand you anything on a silver platter.

When I was in high school, my own desires ran counter to my father's. I wanted to be an actress. I was the star of all our school plays, and I ran a ballet school with a hundred students from the time I was sixteen. I loved the arts, and I knew I was good at it. However, my dad would not hear of it. "Only sluts become actresses!" he told me in a drunken state. I was deeply wounded by that comment; I most certainly did not want to be a slut.

So, I went to university and pursued a different passion: writing and communication. I graduated with an honours degree in English and Communications, and I made both my dad and myself proud.

After university, I got a job writing copy at an advertising agency where I could write for all communication mediums, including print, radio, television, video, direct mail, and transit. I loved writing and producing at large ad agencies – the work was wonderful but also physically demanding. I remember working on television commercials where we filmed all through the night, then going straight into editing the next day to meet both the production and media deadlines. There was little time for a social life.

When I was working on one such television campaign, I hired a woman to help me launch a product. She saw how hard I worked, and when she became the creative director at another advertising agency, she called me and asked me to come and work for her. She said, "I will show you how to work in this business and still have a life." This was a game changer for me. I knew I could not keep up this frantic pace forever, so I joined her agency and she taught me to value a work-life balance. Even today, I still value her mentorship and guidance. Unfortunately, she died of cancer far too young, and I ended up going back to my old ways.

Once I started my own creative communications boutique agency, my habit of overworking returned with a vengeance. I knew I needed an attitude adjustment, and I found one in *A Course in Miracles*. The course teaches that we are so caught up in achieving things that we leave little time for simply being, or for discovering who we truly are within.

When most people sit by themselves and close their eyes, they find their mind racing within their heads. This makes most people feel uncomfortable, and sitting and being quiet for half an hour feels almost unbearable. So, many people start with just a minute or two.

Personally, I don't think you need to meditate for hours, but I do think it is important to learn to quiet our minds and pay attention to what we are thinking.

We need to learn how to still our minds and hear the small voice for God within us all. However, this does not mean we need work at it! *A Course in Miracles* says:

"Nor is a lifetime of contemplation and long periods of meditation
aimed at detachment from the body necessary."

T, 18, VII, 4:9

"When peace comes at last to those who wrestle with temptation
and fight against the giving in to sin;
when the light comes at last into the mind given to contemplation;
or when the goal is finally achieved by anyone, it always comes with just one happy realization;
'I need do nothing'."

T, 18, VII, 5:7

The following turn-around stories look at shifting our perspective on work and career from being outwardly focused (on getting something outside of ourselves) to receiving, accepting, and having gratitude for all that we truly are and have been given by God.

 # Chapter 11

KNOWLEDGE: Where Does It Come From?

Western Thinking
- Knowledge comes from books.

Reverse Thinking
- Knowledge comes from within.

Chapter 11 - Knowledge: Where Does It Come From?
Many of us have been on a search for knowledge. We go to school, to university, and to personal growth courses. But, as *A Course in Miracles* teaches us, the real knowledge most of us needs lies within.

KNOWLEDGE COMES FROM WITHIN:
MY PERSONAL EXPERIENCE WITH THIS REVERSE THOUGHT

In *A Course in Miracles,* knowledge is not taught. Instead it is revealed when you come into alignment with God's way of thinking, which is non-dualistic, timeless, eternal, and loving. The course says that up until the point where we experience this perfectly aligned state, we are in a process of learning. And the way most of us learn on this physical, dualistic level is through comparison.

We compare one way of acting or being with another way. Over time, we have different experiences, and we learn which ones felt good and which ones felt bad. Hopefully, we learn through our personal experiences to choose a loving perception (the right perception or right way of thinking) over a fearful perception (the wrong perception or wrong way of thinking). When we think with right perception, we align with our right minds, and we come from love and light – our bodies literally become vehicles of communication for the divine.

On a practical level, I believe most people have experience with this principle from the time they are young. Here's how it works:
- You are asked to do something by a friend.
- You feel uneasy. Something inside you says, "No."
- However, there is no real logical reason for you to say, "No."
- So, you say, "Yes," because you want them to like you, or you do not like conflict, or whatever other rationale/lies you tell yourself.
- You know what happens next: you do what your friend asks and it goes badly.
- You then say to yourself, *I knew I should have said no.* But, you did it anyways.

In such a scenario, you did not trust your Divine Inner Guidance – your D.I.G. You looked out into the world and saw no reason for saying no, so you said yes! This is how we learn what makes a mis-take.

It has taken me years of practicing and listening within to confirm and follow this inner guidance. I believe the knowledge is always there, but previously I did not listen to my inner wisdom. I acted against what I knew internally because I questioned that voice – I did not trust it. So, I needed experiences to teach me. Here is the story of one such experience.

LISTENING WITHIN

I was in a class where we were doing meditation and visualization. Everyone was lying on mats around the room with their eyes closed. After we went through relaxing all the parts of our body, our instructor asked us to go back in time until we could see ourselves in our mother's womb.

In my visualization, I felt myself connected to my mother. When we were asked to imagine how we were constructing our bodies, I felt like I was building my body out of my mother's pain.

To give you some background, when my mother was pregnant with me, she had left my father because of his drinking. She tried to go live with her mother, but her mother did not sympathize with her situation. She told my mom, "You made your bed. You go lie in it."

My mom was pregnant and distressed, and she did not know where to turn for help. So, she went back to my dad and hid her sadness deep within.

When the visualization ended, we were told to come back to the awareness of the room. Once we all sat up on our mats, our instructor asked each of us to share what we had learned. Some people said amazing things like, "I built my body out of my mom's laughter. Being in the womb was like being in a glass of champagne bubbles, it was magnificent." Wow! I was blown away. What a different experience from my story. As I listened to other people explain what they experienced in their visualization, I got more and more self-conscious about my story. When I finally shared my experience, I felt very timid. Our instructor looked at me sensitively and said, "Diane, we need to talk privately. Talk to me after class and we will set up an individual appointment."

Oh no! That sounds bad, I thought. *I wonder why she needs to see me alone?* I was curious to find out what she thought, though, so I made an appointment to see her the next day.

When I arrived for my appointment, I was told we were going to do Gestalt. My instructor put two pillows on a rug on the floor and explained that we were going to simulate a conversation with my mother. "Here's how it works," she said "You are going to sit on one pillow with your eyes shut and be yourself. Then, I will help you move to the other pillow – the one facing you. On this pillow, you will pretend to be your mother. What's her name?"

"Her name is May," I said.

"Okay," she resumed. "While you are sitting here on the first pillow, you can ask May any question you want. Then, when you move to the other pillow, you must answer the question as if you were your mother. Throughout this whole exercise, it is important to keep your eyes shut – both when you are sitting on a pillow, and when you move. Any questions?"

I did not have any, so our Gestalt session began. The facilitator directed me to ask my mother the question I most wanted the answer to.

I asked my mom, "Why do you not love me?"

The facilitator then helped me move to the other pillow. "Now you are your mother," she said. "May, your daughter Diane is on the other pillow. Can you please answer Diane's question? She wants to know why you do not love her."

To my surprise, I found myself acting as my mother and saying, "I do love you as much as I can. I am not the same as you. I hold myself back from affection. I give you as much as I can."

Again, my facilitator got me to change pillows, then repeated to me what I had said when I was acting as my mother. "Diane, your mother says she does love you as much as she can. What is your response?"

Surprisingly, I believed my mother's answer. It made sense to me. And so the conversation continued, with me questioning my mother and then answering every concern from my mother's viewpoint. This was all done with my eyes closed.

After about an hour, I told my mother, "You need to let me go!"

At that point, I felt the end of a twisted towel being placed in my hands. The other end of the twisted towel was being tugged. My facilitator (now playing my mother) said, "I will never let you go. You are my daughter. I will never let you go!" She tugged the towel towards herself.

I argued, "You must let me go!" I pulled the towel back towards myself.

Before 1 knew it, I was in a tug-a-war with my facilitator/mother. I wanted her to let go, but she continuously stated that I was her daughter, and that she would never let me go.

The tugging on the towel intensified. Soon, I was being dragged around the room shouting at my facilitator/mother, louder and louder, "You must let me go."

"I will never let go!" came the stubborn, insistent answer.

"You must let me go!" I cried, as I was being dragged across the floor. By this point, I was sweating and angry.

"Let me go," I screamed. "Never," she screamed back.

"Let me go. I demand you let me go!" Then, suddenly, brilliantly, I heard a voice within me clearly say, *You can let go.*

I can let go? What an amazing idea. I did not need to hang on and scream anymore. In that moment, I realized this is a two-sided battle, and all I needed to do is let my end of the towel go. And so I did.

The battle with my mom was over. I lay on the floor, exhausted but exhilarated. I finally understood what letting go really means.

When I opened my eyes, my facilitator and I talked about my experience. I was filled with wonder at how easy it was to let go, and how the control was truly in my own hands – not in the hands of someone else. This realization was enlightening for me!

My facilitator told me to take some quiet time, go walk in nature and really let the experience sink in. She told me to be gentle with myself and cherish what I had just learned.

This session was a life-altering experience.

Over the years, many people and self-help books told me that I needed to let go of things. However, it was not until that transformative moment that I lived through a felt experience in my body of how to actually accomplish that task.

Before, I "wanted" to let go, but deep inside I was not letting go. In the end, reading all those self-help books was not helping. I was still battling with my mom – she pulled one way, I pulled the other. However, I can honestly say I did not see my part in the struggle. I was only focused on what my mother should do, not on what I should do. Once I saw my part, the answer to the struggle was easy. Eureka! It is as simple as the books said: "Just let go!" The part I never got until now was, "Stop demanding your mother let go."

This knowledge of what to do came when I listened to my inner voice. Before the Gestalt session, I kept insisting my mother needed to let go of me. What I learned was that in truth, I was the one holding on. I had to let go.

No matter how many books I had read or how many conversations I had had, this knowledge was only something I knew in my head. After I had this experience, I felt what to do right through my entire body and straight into my heart. The truth resonated in every fibre of my being.

HOW DO YOU KNOW WHEN YOU KNOW?

I love what *A Course in Miracles* has to say about truth seeking: *"You know when you stop having to ask questions."*

I no longer had to ask questions about how to get my mom to let go of me. Instead, I took responsibility of the situation. I knew. I let go.

All my inner questions had been answered. I felt free.

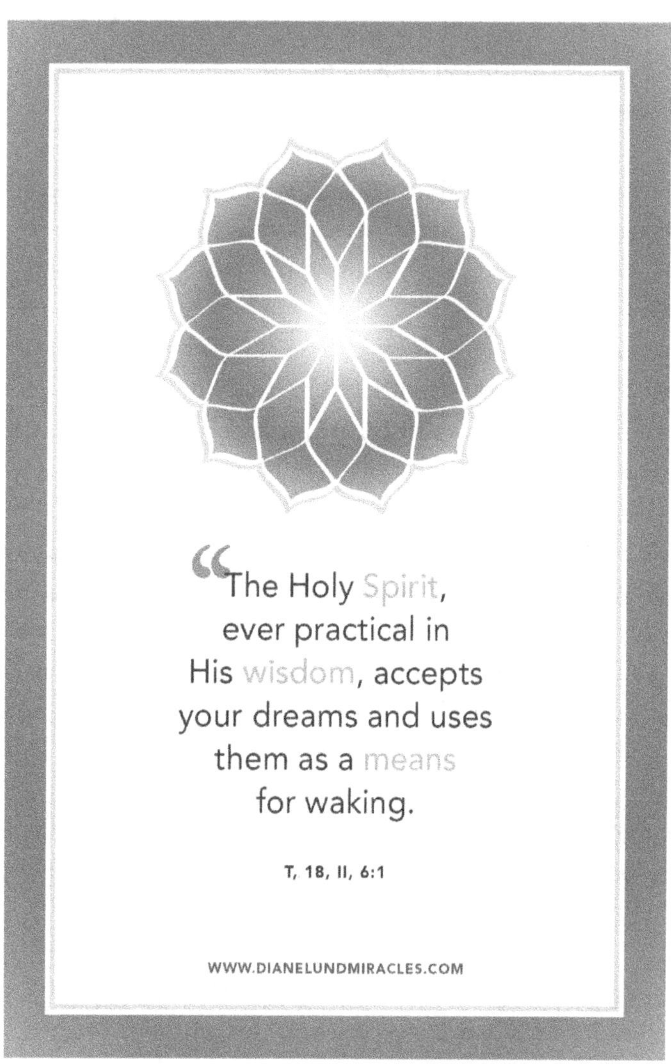

WHAT DOES *A COURSE IN MIRACLES* SAY ABOUT KNOWLEDGE?

In our Western world, we are taught that we can find knowledge in books, and this is certainly a good place to start. I read many self-help books, and several of them had told me I needed to learn to let go. However, the knowledge of how to let go within myself remained abstract; it was like I knew the principle in my head but had not yet integrated it in my heart and within my being.

I thought the person who really needed to let go was my mom – if she let go, all my problems would be solved. In essence, I did not think I had a responsibility to do something because I thought someone outside of me had to do something. This type of thinking is upside-down thinking.

Thinking others need to change keeps us stuck. We have to discover that the only way real change can happen is when we decide to listen to our inner knowledge and follow its advice. In this story, when I listened to my inner voice (after a lot of outward struggle), it told me I was the one who needed to let go, not my mother. What a relief! I could let go, but I could never make my mother let go. With this realization, I turned the balance of power. Rather than letting the power rest with my mother, I took my power back and regained my freedom.

Many of my students ask how they can tell the voice of the ego from the voice of the Holy Spirit. In my story, my ego voice was demanding someone else take responsibility. In contrast, my inner voice, or the source of all knowledge, instructed me that I was responsible for my actions. When I listened to this inner knowledge and acted on its direction, the struggle immediately ended. I was not at odds with myself. I was aligned with my own inner power, and I felt at peace. When we feel this peace rather than inner conflict, we can be sure we are listening to the knowledge that comes from the altar within.

KNOWLEDGE COMES FROM THE ALTAR WITHIN
"Knowledge comes from the altar within and is timeless because it is certain. To perceive the truth is not the same as to know it."

T, 3, III, 5:12,

KNOWLEDGE IS TIMELESS
"Knowledge is timeless, because certainty is not questionable. You know when you have ceased to ask questions."

T, 3, III, 2:10-11

KNOWLEDGE CANNOT DAWN ON A MIND FULL OF ILLUSIONS

"Knowledge cannot dawn on a mind full of illusions, because truth and illusions are irreconcilable. Truth is whole and cannot be known by part of a mind."

T, 10, IV, 2:5-6

KNOWLEDGE WILL BRING PEACE

"Right perception is necessary before God can communicate directly to His altars, which He established in His Sons. There He can communicate His certainty, and His knowledge will bring peace without question."

T, 3, III, 6:1-2

HIS IS THE REALM OF KNOWLEDGE

"Perception is not an attribute of God. His is the realm of knowledge. Yet He has created the Holy Spirit as the Mediator between perception and knowledge. Without this link with God, perception would have replaced knowledge forever in your mind. With this link with God, perception will become so changed and purified that it will lead to knowledge. That is its function as the Holy Spirit sees it. Therefore, that is its function in truth."

W, L43, 1:1-7

 # Chapter 12

DOING: What Do I Need to Do to Create Change?

Western Thinking

- Do something in the world to create change.

Reverse Thinking

- Undo something in your mind to create change.

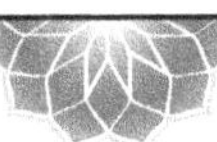

Chapter 12 - Doing: What Do I Need to Do to Create Change?
Do you ever ask yourself, "What can I do to help our ailing world?" Watch this video to discover the power of applying reverse thinking and learn to ask yourself, "What do I need to UNDO in order to create change?"

http://bit.ly/12Change

YOU MUST UNDO SOMETHING IN YOUR MIND TO CREATE CHANGE: MY PERSONAL EXPERIENCE WITH THIS REVERSE THOUGHT

My mother tells me, "You came out of the womb with a long list of things to do." In fact, I stood up and walked at five months old – there was no crawling.

She said, "You always had things to do, people to see," and, she was right in oh-so-many ways. I felt driven to help the world. I pushed myself for good grades. I pushed myself to excellence. I felt sleep was a waste of time. I never felt like I got enough done in a day. These feelings did not change for a long time. The following is a story about when it first dawned on me that perhaps "doing more" was not the answer.

GROWING IN THE GARDEN

I believe relationships are the crucible where most of our real learning takes place, and this has certainly been the case in my own life. One day, while I was at a boyfriend's home, he explained that he had bought his house because it had a beautiful garden that he knew I would like. But, he complained, "You never garden."

I was taken aback.

We did not live together, and I did not realize he wanted me to take care of his garden like it was my own. I had certainly helped him in the garden, but it appeared he wanted me to step up and take the lead.

I was shocked, but I said, "Okay, I will tend to your garden." And with that, I set out on a mission. I looked around the yard and made notes about what plants I thought the garden could use. Then, I went to the gardening store and bought all the plants, soil, and fertilizer I would need. Back at home, I gardened like a fiend. I would show him! He would have an amazing garden. Full of determination, I dug the beds and fertilized them. I pulled the weeds and trimmed the hedges and trees. Then, I started planting.

It was summer at the time, and while the sun did not go down until 9:00 p.m. or later, I still managed to find myself gardening in the dark. It got to the point that I was beginning to have trouble differentiating between the sticks and the slugs! Suddenly exhausted, I sat back on my heels and started to laugh as I thought to myself, *What am I doing? What am I trying to prove?*

Upon reflection, a thought occurred to me: *This is NOT about gardening.*

My boyfriend had said he was unhappy with me because I did not do enough gardening. But last week, it was something else he was unhappy with. And the week before that, it was something different.

No, this was not about how much I gardened or not – this was about my boyfriend feeling like he did not have enough. It occurred to me that he wanted me to fill a hole, not in the garden, but inside himself.

Like a bolt of lightning, I suddenly realized that whatever I did on the outside would never be enough to fill him up on the inside. In an instant of true clarity, I knew with certainty that I could never do enough to please him.

What a thought! What liberation! I put down my gardening tools and laughed at myself.

You have to fix the problem at the source, I thought to myself. The problem is not the garden – the problem is thinking something is wrong, thinking from lack. I realized my boyfriend was blaming me for the things he believed made him feel bad, and I always tried to fix the problem out in the world. But now, it was dawning on me that the problem was clearly not out in the world. The source of this problem was in my mind, and in my boyfriend's mind.

When we project our inner lack out into the world, we see the lack as being outside ourselves. We then try to fix the problem where we think it is located. In this case, I thought the problem was the garden and my lack of tending it. But the real problem was not located in a garden, or in another person – the problem was really in my head and in my thinking.

For years, I had thought I just had to do more and achieve more to make my boyfriend, my parents, and my teachers happy. Then, I would be a success. Now, though, I realized I was mistaken. What I really had to do was to undo my thinking about the problem and discover where the real source of the problem existed. Here's another story that helps to illustrate the idea.

LIFE IS LIKE A MOVIE PROJECTOR

Imagine you are watching a movie and you don't like what you see up on the screen. So, you go up to the screen and start screaming at the images to change.

Of course, the images do not change. The movie keeps playing and the images keep on showing up in the same way. It does not matter what you are doing in front of the screen. You can yell all you want; the images are set.

If we want the images on the screen of our physical world to change, we need to go up to the projector room and change the film. Think of the projector room like your mind, while movie playing is composed of the thoughts that keep going round and round in your head.

Yelling at the screen (or yelling at the images we see in the world) does not help. If we want to change what we see, we need to get to where the images are created – both in our individual mind. and in the one mind we all share. Both our personal thoughts and our collective thoughts get projected out into the world, meaning we literally see our thoughts on the screen of our three-dimensional world.

Here's the big mistake: we try to outwardly change the images that we see when their source is inward. We must turn within and change our thoughts if we want to see something different projected out into our physical world.

WHAT HOLDS US BACK?
We believe we are weak, or small, or insignificant, or powerless when exactly the opposite is true: we are all an extension of God. Together, we are "the one son." We are all eternal, timeless love that has the power to extend and create, just like God. However, we are scared to admit we have this awesome power, because then we will have to admit that we have created the situations we find ourselves in. It is easier to blame, criticize, and stay small. If we believe we have power, worth, and knowledge, we must own that we are creating our world!

No one else is creating our world. We are. This is the true knowledge that scares us!

I believe we are frightened of our own power and magnificence. We have blocked the knowledge of our own creative power from our minds by thinking wrongly about ourselves. What we really need is not to do more in the world, but to undo our thinking about the world and ourselves.

WHAT DOES *A COURSE IN MIRACLES* SAY ABOUT UNDOING?

The North American culture is all about doing, whereas *A Course in Miracles* is all about undoing. The world is not to be blamed any more than your mother, your boyfriend, your boss, or the environment. The world is neutral – an outward projection of what we all carry in our one united mind. It is up to each of us to decide for ourselves what we see.

- If you think what you see is bad, you will act accordingly.
- If you think what you see is good, you will act accordingly.

However, the physical images you see are truly illusionary – that is, they shift and change. They are not eternal. Everyone sees the same images and then has different thoughts about them.

You may try to change the external world to gain a sense of control, but it is only by changing your internal world that you have control. You don't have control over what others think or do, but you do have control over what you think and do. So, it follows that what needs to be corrected is not what is outside of ourselves. We do not need to change the world; we need to change our mind about the world. The error is in our own minds.

We don't need to do more in the world. Instead, we need to undo the errors in our thinking so that who we truly are will shine like a magnificent light within our minds. Then, whatever we do will be in alignment with who we truly are: love eternal.

UNDO ERROR AT ALL LEVELS

"A major step in the Atonement plan is to undo error at all levels."

T, 2, IV, 2:1

PREPARE NOW FOR THE UNDOING

"Prepare you now for the undoing of what never was. If you already understood the difference between truth and illusion, the Atonement would have no meaning. The holy instant, the holy relationship, the Holy Spirit's teaching, and all the means by which salvation is accomplished would have no purpose. For they are all but aspects of the plan to change your dreams of fear to happy dreams, from which you waken easily to knowledge. Put yourself not in charge of this, for you cannot distinguish between advance and retreat. Some of your greatest advances you have judged as failures, and some of your deepest retreats you have evaluated as success."

T, 18, V, 1:1-6

THE MEANS FOR UNDOING

"God wills no one suffer. He does not will anyone to suffer for a wrong decision, including you. That is why He has given you the means for undoing it. Through His power and glory all your wrong decisions are undone completely, releasing you and your brother from every imprisoning thought any part of the Sonship holds. Wrong decisions have no power, because they are not true."

T, 8, III, 7:5-9

THE HOLY SPIRIT HAS THE TASK OF UNDOING WHAT THE EGO MADE

"The Holy Spirit has the task of undoing what the ego has made. He undoes it at the same level on which the ego operates, or the mind would be unable to understand the change."

T, 5, III, 5:5-6

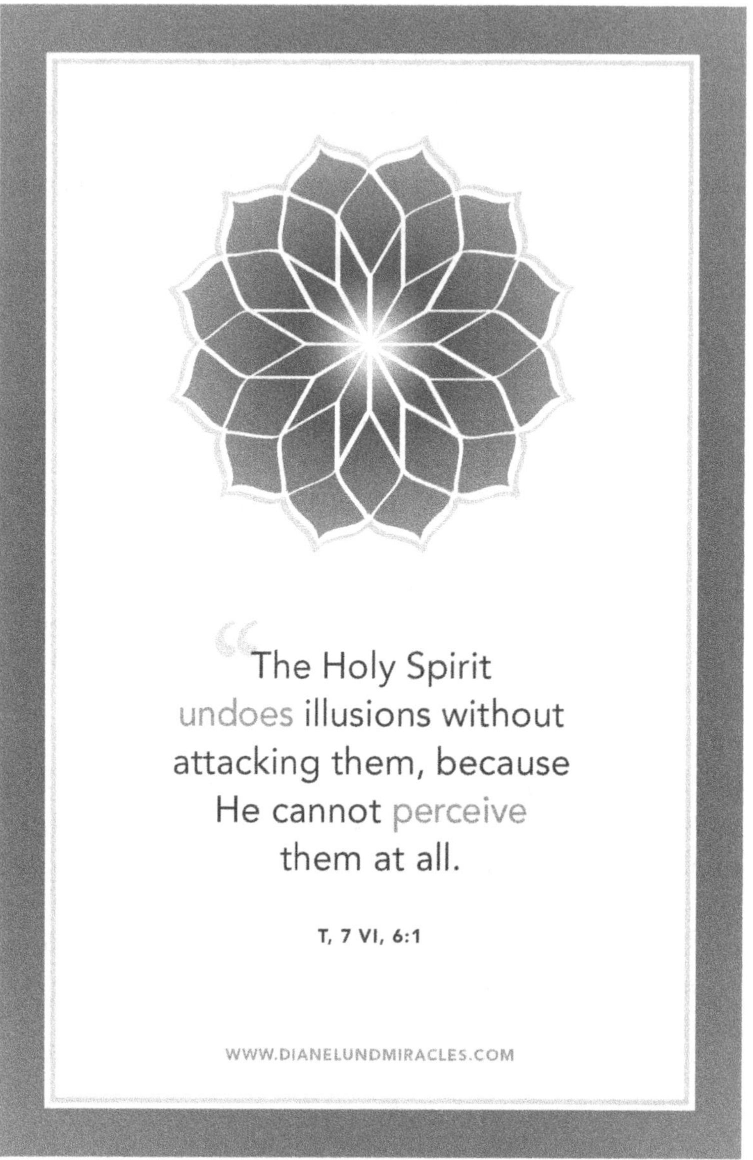

Chapter 13

WORTH: Where Do I Find It?

Western Thinking

- I prove my worth by getting money, awards, and achievements.

Reverse Thinking

- My worth needs no worldly proof; it is my birthright.

Chapter 13 - Worth: Where Do I Find It?

How do you define your worth? Do you base it on the things you own, on accolades or competitions you've won, or on other people's opinions of you? *A Course in Miracles* teaches us that to be or feel worthy, you do not need to prove anything. Watch the video to find out why you never need to prove your worth.

http://bit.ly/13Worth

MY WORTH NEEDS NO WORLDLY PROOF; IT IS MY BIRTHRIGHT
MY PERSONAL EXPERIENCE WITH THIS REVERSE THINKING

Generally, the Western world measures our worth by what we receive. Did we receive the promotion, a degree, the job, the money, or an exotic vacation? *A Course in Miracles* flips this concept on its head. It says your worth has nothing to do with what you get or receive in life. Instead, it says God establishes your worth. It is intrinsic. It is your birthright.

- What does this mean?
- How is our worth built into our being?
- Why is this an important concept for us to explore?

Here's my story about personal worth.

I JUST WANTED TO PLEASE MY PARENTS!
I am sure this story is true for so many of us. When we are little, our parents rule our worlds. What they say goes, and their desires for us carry a big weight. As we often have no other parents to compare their behaviour to, we believe that what our parents do and tell us is good and true, right down to silly little things.

I remember my parents telling me, "Do not swallow the seeds in your apple, or else a tree will grow inside of you." The image was absolutely startling. I could imagine the roots extending down my legs, the trunk pushing up through my stomach, and the branches reaching up for the light through my eyes and mouth. I had a vivid imagination. I was petrified, and I argued with my parents out of my fear, "No, that can't be true." However, they assured me that it was. I started to worry, because I had swallowed seeds!

- How long would it take?
- Would I survive?
- How would I know the tree was growing?

Of course, my parents were just pulling my leg. However, I was young, innocent, and trusting, and I did not want trees growing inside of me. I also wanted my parents to love me, and that meant doing what they said.

My parents struggled with their world of money, family, and addiction – there were secrets we could not share. Even as a young child, it was obvious to me that that they did not need any more problems. I thought that was why they fought every night: they just had too many of them. They needed me to behave so I would not become just another problem in their troubled lives.

Unfortunately, it turned out that "behaving" was way more difficult to achieve than I initially thought. My mother was often worn out in the morning from a night of fighting with my dad. Since I was the oldest, it became my job to help my mom with the everyday tasks of getting a household moving. But no matter what I did, I just did not do it right. When she wanted me to cut sandwiches, I cut them the wrong way. When she wanted me to get dressed, I put on the wrong clothes. When she needed me to find her wedding ring (that she had taken off in a fit of rage the night before) and I could not find it, she complained, "You are a miserable girl…good for nothing." All this just made me try harder. I believed I could learn what my mom wanted and perform accordingly so that she would be proud of me. However, every day it seemed she changed the goal posts. One day she talked about reincarnation, but when I brought it up the next day, she said, "Don't talk about such things. They do not exist. Don't be a silly girl." Or she might say, "Don't kiss the boys." But when I came home from a party and told her I refrained from playing spin the bottle, she replied, "Silly you. You missed all the fun!"

I grew up being very confused about how to please my mother. On the bright side, I think that is how I honed my inner abilities. I needed to pick up on even the slightest change in mood, vibration, or behaviour. I grew invisible antennae – I was always scanning the environment. What was up today? I got good at picking up subtle changes and knowing what they meant. If I said the wrong thing, my mom would wash my mouth out with soap, refusing to let me wash my mouth out afterwards. It was extremely unpleasant. Or, she would chase me around the house with the wooden spoon, calling me names. I would run and lock myself in the bathroom, too terrified to come out. Obviously, what I was doing wasn't working. I just seemed to disappoint her at every turn.

GO FIGURE
I remember going to skating lessons and trying to skate a figure eight into the ice. You needed to use the outside or inside blade edge on your skates very carefully to make the necessary turns. My instructor was watching, and I kept missing it. I kept apologizing over and over.

Finally, he took me aside and told me to please stop apologizing. There was nothing to be sorry for – I wasn't doing anything wrong. However, it was obvious to me that I wasn't doing anything right either. I wanted to get it! I wanted to make the perfect figure eight so I could get the skating badge. I wanted to make my parents proud of me. I wanted to show them that someone thought I was good at something.

Unfortunately, this pattern of trying to please people continued for years. I just did not get it. I worked so hard to get good grades, to win scholastic awards and athletic badges.

I loved dancing as a child, and I practised hard to be the best ballet dancer, the best actor, the best performer. Sadly, my parents often did not come to my shows. My dad was frequently out drinking, and for a long time my mom had no car to get to the shows. So, they did not see me dance, or act, or perform on stage very often. I felt defeated by their absence. All that work, all those rehearsals, just did not help.

My home life was rapidly going down the tubes as my dad continued to drink heavily and my mom paid the price in nightly verbal abuse. I was becoming disillusioned with the world. It did not deliver the dream just pain and loneliness. I did not know what to do – it seemed that working harder was not working!

My mother told me in no uncertain terms, "Do not talk about what goes on in our home to anyone. Be a good girl, keep your mouth shut." And so I did. I did not tell anyone that I was aching inside. I called myself the Queen of Melancholy, and I sat in my room and played sad songs on my recorder player.

CHEMISTRY EXPLOSION

The first time I told anyone what was going on for me, I totally surprised myself by telling my Grade Eleven chemistry teacher. Go figure! I barely knew him. I had tried to do my chemistry homework the night before, but my parents were fighting so loudly that I could not concentrate. Eventually, I went to bed and woke up early to do the work when my parents were asleep. I did not finish on time and ended up late for school. When I went into the chemistry room to hand in my homework, my teacher said I was late and he was not going to accept it. Suddenly and without warning, I burst into angry tears and sobbed out the whole ugly story to this man who I didn't even know. He sat back in his chair, his eyes wide, and just looked at me as if he saw me for the very first time. He seemed to realize I was an animal he had never seen before – an oddity, an out-of-the-box thing that was totally bewildering. When I finally calmed down and sat down, he looked at me and asked me where I normally sat in his class.

He said, "Where? Show me."

I got up and showed him. "From now on," he said, "you will sit here," moving my class placement to the front of the room. "I will take care of you," he said.

"Please, please do not tell anyone," I begged, "Please do not tell my parents I said something, they will be so mad." He looked at me and said "No, I will not say anything. But I want YOU to say something. If this happens again, you just let me know. I will understand." I broke into sobs and cried as if my heart was breaking. I couldn't believe it – someone was going to understand. I did not have to hide everything anymore.

I felt a strange sort of relief and guilt flood over me. Guilt because I had not been the good girl, and I knew on some level my parents would feel I had betrayed them; relief because I had stated my truth for the very firt time, and someone actually understood. It meant a lot.

For a long time I was puzzled by what happened. *Why did I tell my chemistry teacher, of all people?* I was certainly in no way close to him or knew him personally. But that was just the way it was: an explosion of emotion in an impersonal chemistry lab.

I wish I could say that things changed from then on, but of course life is not that simple. A lifetime of being a people pleaser was not going to shift overnight or with one personal reveal. It was going to take a long time and a lot of serious work to shift the life pattern I had developed. My saving grace was I knew something was wrong. I knew I wanted to feel differently. I knew I needed help, and I was driven to find it.

A decade or so later I went to a place called The Haven to take some personal growth courses, and there I bumped up against this issue once more. My teachers told me it is called being "field dependent." I was looking outside of myself for approval, for love, for worthiness. I wanted proof that I measured up and was good enough. I hated to admit it, but I knew that was exactly what I was doing. I was scanning my environment and trying to do what was expected of me so I could prove I was worthy of acceptance and love. However, my eyes were beginning to open and my heart was willing to change. I just needed to open the door for inner guidance and inner wisdom.

WE ALL KNOW THE TRUTH

I believe we all know the truth of who we are – we have just covered it up with all kinds of lies about ourselves. Lies like:

- I am not good enough.
- I am not clever enough.
- I am not pretty enough.
- I am not athletic enough.
- I am not.

We think we know these things about ourselves because of our past experiences. We believe we are the authority on who we are, but we are not. We did not create our authentic essence – our inner spirit. God extended his eternal love to create his "one son," which is everyone. We were made from perfect love because our Creator is only perfect love.

All the other things we say about ourselves –"I'm too old, too bald, too tall, too short" – are judgments that really say to God, "I know better than you. I know who I am, and I am flawed!" When we do this, when we say words about ourselves that are not true, we are listening to the ego – the voice for separation – and not to our inner guidance, the Holy Spirit that is the voice for God.

It never works to try and get your feeling of self-worth from things, degrees, awards, money, status or fame. It is not that these things are wrong or bad on any level, but when we think these things will prove we are worth, we will be truly disappointed. As the old saying goes, "I was looking for love in all the wrong places."

I was looking for love through achievement. I wanted other people to see I was good and consequently love me, but the love I was looking for – the love I so desperately craved – did not reside outside of myself.

Finding our true, authentic worth comes from looking within. Our true worth isn't something we need to prove to anybody; our worth was established the minute we were created. We are all born from endless, unchanging love. Our spirit, our very essence, is this pure love. The fact of the matter is that your worth is intrinsic; it is your birthright. Because you are born from pure love, you *are* pure love. You do not need to do anything to have it because it is your natural inheritance. It never shifts, and it never changes. It simply is, and it is yours for the finding. It is the treasure within. It is the gold we all seek.

The question, then, is this: do you have to the courage to look within to find it?

WHAT DOES *A COURSE IN MIRACLES* SAY ABOUT WORTH?

How do we discover our own inner worth? For me, the formula could be put down to **listen, learn, and do**. We have to make a decision to not let the sounds of the outside world dominate our thinking. Stop letting other people tell you who you are or what you should do. Instead, start making a daily commitment to listen to your inner world. Everyone needs to develop their intuitive gifts. We need to listen within and learn to distinguish between "The Voice for God" and "The Voice for the Ego." This is, for most people, a lifelong practise.

Generally, the ego is driven by fear and responds by defending, attacking, blaming or withdrawing, to mention just a few of its tactics. In contrast, the Holy Spirit comes from love and forgiveness, and it wants to join with others. The ego separates while The Holy Spirit asks for you to heal the separation between you and others.

HERE IS A BIG SECRET

You are always doing one thing or the other. In every moment you are listening to the Voice for the Ego or the Voice for Love. You are always choosing which internal guide you want to follow. Do you want to turn on the voice of fear and feed it with stories that seem to make it real and scary? Or, will you turn to the voice for love? *A Course in Miracles* is very clear about this:

> *"You are much too tolerant of mind wanderings*
> *and are passively condoning your mind's miscreations.*
> *The particular result does not matter, but the fundamental error does.*
> *The correction is always the same.*
> *Before you choose to do anything, ask me if your choice is in accord with mine.*
> *If you are sure that it is, there will be no fear."*
>
> T, 2, VI, 4:6-10

How you think is your decision in each and every moment. Everyone has built a unique story, and the way to dissolve all the limiting beliefs you have about yourself starts with a simple willingness to try to think in a new way. You do not have to believe this new way will work, but you do have to have some faith that there is something greater than yourself which has your best interest at heart. And, you have to listen for that advice, guidance, and direction. Learn to follow it, no matter what, then do what it asks.

> *"The truth is that you are responsible for what you think,*
> *because it is only at this level that you can exercise choice.*
> *What you do comes from what you think.*
> *You cannot separate yourself from the truth by 'giving' autonomy to behavior."*
>
> T, 2, VI, 2:6-8

In other words, your behaviour (winning awards, accolades, giving money, etc.) cannot take the place of truly knowing and embracing the truth about yourself.

THERE IS NO MAGIC BULLET

You must change your mind. Worth does not come from things, but rather from the knowledge of who you truly are within your essence or spirit. Your work in this physical realm is to learn to train your mind to transform what you see in the world. Remember, you are always listening to one thought system or the other. You can think with the Holy Spirit as your guide, or you can think with fear and let your Ego be your guide. You choose in every moment.

> *"You must change your mind, not your behavior,*
> *and this is a matter of willingness.*
> *You do not need guidance except at the mind level.*
> *Correction belongs only at the level where change is possible.*
> *Change does not mean anything at the symptom level where it cannot work."*
>
> T, 2, VI, 3:4-7

So, this means changing jobs, changing locations, changing partners, or upgrading your car does not work. These things and words mean nothing; only the application of this material to your life truly matters. You must put the principles into practise. You must train your mind. You will believe this truth only when you experience the transformation for yourself. That is what happened for me.

The first step was acknowledging that my way of going through life was not working. I wanted another way. I went to a study group for *A Course in Miracles* because the language and the principles were just too difficult for me to learn on my own. When my teacher moved away, I could not find a study group I enjoyed in my area. So, I started my own. I met with a core group of about ten people for almost twenty years before I decided to create a Meetup group and put it out on the Internet. Now, there are over two hundred and fifty people that have registered for my group. I trust that each and every one is on their chosen path and will be led as I have been led.

This book is my story of how I put *A Course In Miracles'* principles into practise in my daily life. I can tell you from the depth of my heart that has not always been easy. I did not always easily accept these ideas or believe they would transform my life. But then, shift happened! And once I saw the many shifts, I wanted more! I wanted to feel that joy and that happiness on a daily basis, and that is what I want for you as well. Believe me, I know it is not always easy to change your mind, but you are worth the effort. You are worth the time. You are worth it.

YOUR WORTH IS ESTABLISHED BY GOD

"Your worth is not established by teaching or learning. Your worth is established by God. As long as you dispute this everything you do will be fearful, particularly any situation that lends itself to the belief in superiority and inferiority."

T, 4, I, 7:1-3

NOTHING YOU DO OR THINK IS NECESSARY TO ESTABLISH YOUR WORTH

"Again – nothing you do or think or wish or make is necessary to establish your worth. This point is not debatable except in delusions. Your ego is never at stake because God did not create it. Your spirit is never at stake because He did."

T, 4, I, 7:6-10

TO HAVE, GIVE ALL TO ALL

"The Holy Spirit communicates only what each one can give to all. He never takes anything back, because he wants you to keep it. Therefore, His teaching begins with this lesson: to have, give all to all."

T, 6, A, 5:10-13

REVERSING OUR PERCEPTION AND TURNING IT RIGHT SIDE UP

"This is a very preliminary step, and the only one you must take for yourself. It is not even necessary that you complete the step yourself, but it is necessary that you turn in that direction. Having chosen to go that way, you place yourself in charge of the journey, where you and only you must remain. This step may appear to exacerbate conflict rather than resolve it, because it is the beginning step in reversing our perception and turning it right side up. This conflicts with the upside-down perception you have not yet abandoned or the change in direction would not be necessary."

T, 6, A, 6:1-5

LOVE ENTERS ANY MIND THAT TRULY WANTS IT

"Love will immediately enter into any mind that truly wants it, but it must want it truly. This means that it wants it without the ego's drive to get."

T, 4, III, 4:7-8

PERFECT LOVE IS IN YOU!

"You have so little faith in yourself because you are unwilling to accept the fact that perfect love is in you. And so you seek without for what you cannot find without."

T, 15, VI, 2:1-2

 # Chapter 14

ANSWERS: Who Has the Answers?

Western Thinking
- Rely on yourself for answers.

Reverse Thinking
- Rely on God for answers.

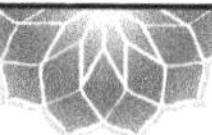

Chapter 14 - Answers: Who Has the Answers?

Who has the answers? You? Your friends? The government? It's difficult to know. Watch this video to discover how *A Course in Miracles* has taught me to find the answers to my most burning questions.

http://bit.ly/14Answers

RELY ON GOD FOR THE ANSWERS:
MY PERSONAL EXPERIENCE WITH THIS REVERSE THINKING

All my life, I have had headaches. I have read the Louise Hay book *You Can Heal Your Life* and her chart at the back of the book says headaches are a sign of invalidating the self. They represent self-criticism and fear. Now, when I have a headache, I ask myself:

- What am I feeling bad about?
- What am I feeling guilty about?
- What do I fear?

Most times I can answer these questions, but often I cannot. So, I take my unanswerable questions to my inner teacher. Here's what I discovered about my headaches.

THE WORLD IS ON MY SHOULDERS

In my mind, I always meet my inner teacher, Jesus, in a beautiful garden. I simply close my eyes and imagine I am there with him. The garden is a Mediterranean garden full of raised beds planted with citrus trees, flowers, and fragrant herbs. Jesus and I often sit on a bench under the fragrant trees to talk. One day, during my meditation, I asked him, *Why do I have so many headaches?*

In my vision, Jesus said to me. *You doubt yourself and your abilities. You question whether or not you can handle a situation or a project. This is the ego's ploy – to think that you have to handle a situation or a project. This puts everything on your shoulders, and your head hurts with the responsibility you feel. This is a wrong perception. Instead of thinking:*

EVERYTHING IS UP TO ME,
simply shift the word,
ME to THEE!
Then the message is:
EVERYTHING IS UP TO THEE!

I laughed out loud. Of course that's the answer. Instead of trying to solve problems myself, I had to hand over my problems to the one who truly knows: the Holy Spirit.

Remember, problems are illusionary. The mind makes them up to keep you occupied and turned away from your true reality – your perfection in God. If you learn to turn to the Holy Spirit and hand over all your problems and worries, this will take the pressure and weight off your shoulders.

Instead of relying on your own strength, rely on the strength of the Holy Spirit.

The next time you have a problem, instead of saying, "It's up to me," say "It's up to thee," and then let go and let the Holy Spirit handle it. This is such a fabulous lesson!

Upon reflection, I realized I do take things on. I think I have to solve things instead of handing things over to the Holy Spirit, who uses everything for good. Today, I remember this simple lesson as, **"NOT ME: THEE!"**

When I think this, I remember who I truly am: not a pile of problems but a daughter of God, whole, perfect and complete. I cannot go wrong when I align with what is whole/holy in me.

THE AUTHORITY PROBLEM

According to *A Course in Miracles*, when we believe we can sort things out and we don't ask for help, we have an **authority problem**. We believe that we are the authority on the issue, not the Holy Spirit. This is an upside-down and backwards way of thinking. Here's how we got to this backwards thinking.

The real authority of the universe is God. From God (eternal love, or Source) everything else extended in perfect wholeness. This extension of God is the one son of God (invisible, eternal love), with the power to create just like God. The only difference is God is the real authority, the father of everything. When this one son of God asked, "Is there something more than this?" separation was born and a split in the mind occurred. We went from being one with God (being in one mind) to making a decision without God (being in a split mind). We became a decision maker. We decided to think without God.

We thought that maybe there was something more than God, so we left the one mind and became a split mind. Then the ego emerged from deep within the split mind. The ego is the part of the mind that believes in separation from God. It thought, *Perhaps God will be mad if we think separately from him.* This separation thought made us feel deeply uncomfortable, so we projected what we did not want – fear and guilt – out of our minds and created a world that reflected our split mind: the world of duality, the world of illusion.

As this process happened (from being one with God, to being a decision maker, to having a split mind, to the birth of our ego), we slowly began to forget where we originated from and why we are here. Instead, we listened to the ego, which said, *God will be mad you separated from him,* and, *We need to hide. Come with me and we can create a world different from God's world, where you get what God can never give you. You can be special.*

We all thought that being special sounded interesting. However, no one is special in God's world because we are one and are all the same. Everyone is the same eternal love, abundance, and joy.

We liked the idea of being special, so we chose to listen to the ego. When we did this, we projected thoughts of separation and specialness. The course says these thoughts of separation created physical bodies. According to *A Course in Miracles*, the body is literally the thought of separation made manifest. When we think we are a body and not a spirit, we move away from our true identity. We literally forgot where we came from, and we forgot who we are – the eternal sons and daughters of God. Instead, we put ourselves in charge of our lives.

We think we know best. Perhaps we deny the existence of God, or maybe we just question it. We live thinking that we, not God, are the ultimate authority. We turn away from listening to our inner spirit and towards listening to the physical world. If you are feeling sad, frustrated, depressed, discouraged, or any other negative emotion, this could be a sign that you have an authority problem. The good news is that it is easy to correct. You simply need to start handing your problems over to the universe, or God, or your higher power. I don't really care what you call it.

I have truly learned: It's not up to ME, it is literally up to THEE!

When we turn our thinking on its head like this, we align with our own inner power as well as the awesome power of the universe, and what is hard becomes easy. Here's a story from my life that clearly illustrates this principle.

GOD IS IN THE AIR!
I had a dream where I was asked to learn to fly a sail in the air. The instructor showed me how, but when it came to my turn, my sail was just flapping in the breeze. I could not seem to catch the wind and my sail kept tumbling back down. Then, I suddenly caught the wind, and I was faced with a steady surge of strong power that I knew would take me quickly and profoundly to my goal.

In my dream, an invisible voice said, *This is what it is like to find the power and strength of God working in your life.* It said:

Remember this feeling.
You are the sail, and the wind is God – invisible, powerful
requiring little to no effort from you.
When you align with this great power, everything is thus done with great ease and joy.
In this way everything you do is effortless.

I wrote this dream down in my miracle journal the year I was studying to be a minister.

A few months later, I was at a writing retreat in Turks and Caicos. I was with a small group of six women who were all there to write books and enjoy the islands. On the first day, one of the girls decided she did not like the look of the place and did not want to stay, which opened up space for someone on the island to take her spot. The publisher who was running the retreat had just given a talk on the island, and a couple of people had expressed interest in joining our group.

The next day, a new girl joined us who lived on the island and taught kite boarding. I did not think anything of it until a day or two later when she decided she wanted to show us what she did. On her demonstration day, she showed us what it takes to fly a kite in the air and then sail on a board across the ocean. Suddenly, she began saying almost the same thing as the voice in my dream: "You have to find the wind direction and then not fight the wind. You have to align with this great power and just let the wind take you. When you do, you will find kite boarding requires almost no effort."

Wow! My dream was actually reinforcing itself in my physical world. It truly blew me away. It is up to me to align myself with the great universal power, and then to let go and fly.

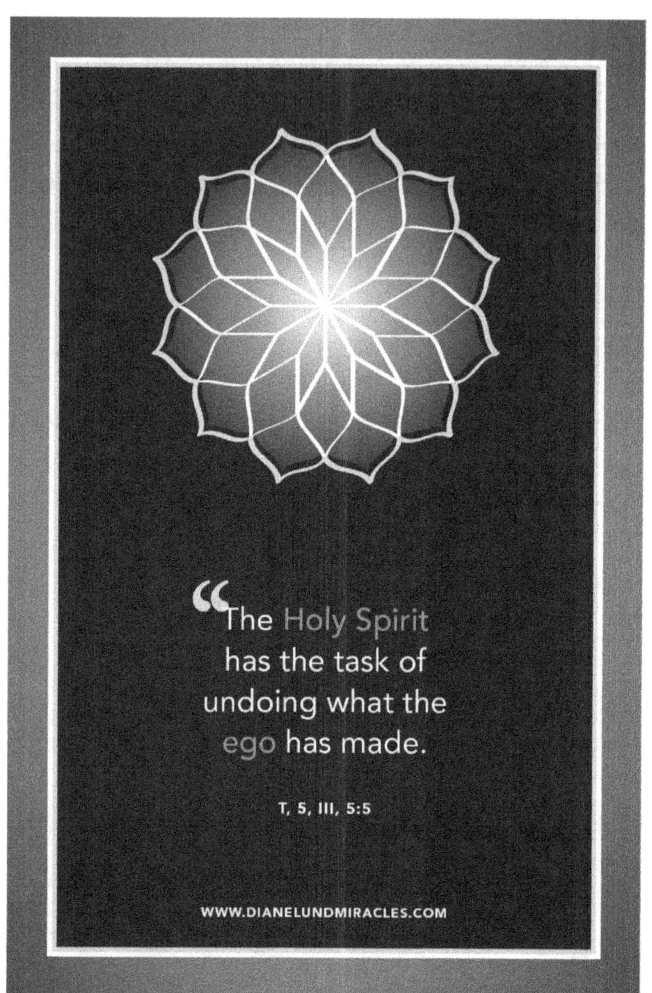

WHAT DOES *A COURSE IN MIRACLES* SAY ABOUT ANSWERS?

Who has the answers to our problems?
- Do we want our politicians to provide the answers?
- Do our parents have the answers?
- What about our teachers and scholars – do they have the answers?

Actually, most people believe *they* have all the answers. We believe we are the authority on most things in our lives, and so we do not want people to tell us what to do. We want to captain our own ship and navigate our own world. However, the problem with this way of thinking is that we put all the pressure on ourselves and, as my story demonstrated, doing so can literally give us headaches. We were not meant to do this alone – we were meant to do this with the assistance of the whole universe. We cannot know everything, and what a joy it is to hand the reins over to someone who does know.

The Holy Spirit is the communication link to God or eternal love, and this power can do so much more and organize so much more than we ever could alone. It is truly miraculous to acknowledge that the authority lies not in our hands or heads, but in our willingness to acknowledge our true heritage as one spirit extended from the eternal love of God. When we do this, we align ourselves with the powerful forces of the universe. It is like aligning ourselves with the power of the wind – it effortlessly takes us where we need to go.

THE AUTHORITY PROBLEM
"The authority problem. This is 'the root of all evil'."

T, 3, VI, 7:2-3

THE QUESTION OF AUTHORSHIP
"The issue of authority is really a question of authorship. When you have an authority problem, it is always because you believe you are the author of yourself and project your delusion onto others."

T, 3, VI, 8:1-2

FUNDAMENTAL QUESTION OF AUTHORSHIP
"Peace is the natural heritage of spirit. Everyone is free to refuse to accept his inheritance, but he is not free to establish what his inheritance is. The problem everyone must decide is the fundamental question of Authorship. All fear comes ultimately, and sometimes by way of very devious routes, from the denial of Authorship. The offense is never to God, but only to those who deny Him. To deny His Authorship is to deny yourself the reason for peace, so that you see yourself only in segments. This strange perception is the authority problem."

T, 3, VI, 10:1-7

YOUR UPSIDE-DOWN PERCEPTION HAS BEEN RUINOUS

"Your upside-down perception has been ruinous to your peace of mind. You have seen yourself in a body and the truth outside you, locked away from your awareness of the body's limitations. Now we are going to try to see this differently.

W, L72, 8:3-5

IT IS THE BODY THAT IS OUTSIDE OF US

"The light of truth is in us, where it was placed by God. It is the body that is outside us, and is not our concern. To be without a body is to be in our natural state. To recognize the light of truth in us is to recognize ourselves as we are."

W, L72, 9:1-4

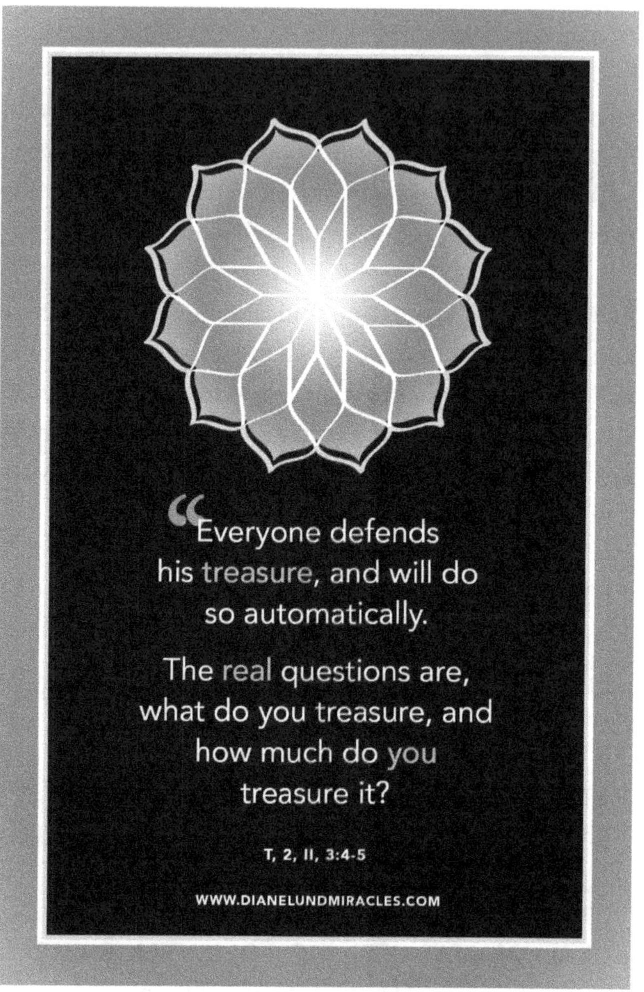

# Chapter 15

WEALTH: Am I Rich or Poor?

Western Thinking
- I am poor without money.

Reverse Thinking
- I am wealthy always.

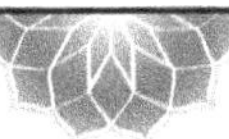

Chapter 15 – Wealth: Am I Rich or Poor? In the Western world we are often obsessed by the question, "Will I have enough money?" Although we may think of our wealth as tied to our monetary worth, *A Course in Miracles* looks at the richness of your spirit. Watch this video to discover how you are already wealthy. http://bit.ly/15Wealth

I AM WEALTHY ALWAYS:
MY PERSONAL EXPERIENCE WITH THIS REVERSE THINKING

Money and finances can be such a huge topic. Money worries are no fun, and I have certainly had my struggles with then. But then I took a course on money and examined my thoughts behind the pieces of paper and discs of metal and what I discovered was illuminating. Here is my story on true wealth.

MY SECRET

When I was a small child, I had a secret: I believed I was extremely rich and wealthy. Somehow, I knew that people would not like it that I possessed so much, so I kept this knowledge secret. I knew I was wealthy, but I did not want people to feel bad if they were not wealthy.

This is the story I told myself.

In reality, I lived in a middle-income household. I can remember my dad building my bed from scratch in our carport. We did not have enough money for a bed, and for the first few months after we had moved into our home, I slept on a mattress on the floor. These logical facts did not seem to matter to me, though. I felt rich inside, and I delighted in it.

THE MONEY GAME

Years later, I took a course on money. They asked us to play a game where we were each given a quarter to spend, and we got to decide whether we would keep the quarter or give it over to play in the game.

Surprisingly, most people wanted to keep their quarter rather than playing the game. Wow – think what that says! Well, the instructors decided to change the rules, and everyone had to give over their quarter to play the game. Then we were divided into groups of eight.

The goal of the game was to explain to the others why you deserved to have all the group's money. When the first round began, I believed I could easily convince my group that I should have all the money. My belief was correct. I moved on to the next round along with the other round-one victors. Round two continued in the same manner: convince your group why should you have all the money.

The game played on until there were just two people standing. We then had to speak to the whole group and explain why we deserved all the money, and the whole group had to listen and then vote on who should be the final victor. I instinctively knew that I could convince everyone to give me their money and win this game because I was going to use the money for something everyone would support. I made my pitch, then the other person made theirs, and in the end I got all the money.

When it was over, one of the leaders said to the group, "It is just a game. It did not matter who won or who did not. What matters," he said, "was how you felt during the game?" The instructors encouraged us to search our hearts and minds and then express to each other during the lunch break what we had felt when we were playing the game.

Lunch came, and with it an assault of emotions. Almost all the men in the room came up to me one by one and told me that they hated me for winning. I was shocked. The women also did not like that I had won the game, but they were not as harsh. I don't remember receiving one positive comment from anyone. So, although I had won, I felt I had lost the affection and love of my friends. I felt incredibly sad.

An old bell sounded deep within my being, long and low. I felt the reverberations of an inner knowing.

I had known I was rich within ever since I was a child, but I also sensed that people would not like that knowledge. I believed they would compare themselves to me, think about what they did not have, and consequently dislike me. Now here I was, experiencing this reality. I had exposed what I knew about myself to the whole room, and I was experiencing the backlash of exposure. I started to shrink and hide.

My inner ego complained, *See, we always knew you needed to hide this fact.*

As I listened to the voice within, I started to truly understand why I did hide a lot of myself from the world. I realized how cruel people can be when you come out on top. *It would have been better to let them win,* I thought to myself. *I prefer being liked to being the one with all the money.*

For me, the interesting learning from that day came after we had played the money game. Suddenly, it became very obvious to me why I let men lead, and why I did not let men fully know what I thought and felt. Surely I would receive the same kind of comments I had received at lunch if I started to talk about my opinions. I started to withdraw into the crowd. *It is dangerous to stand out,* I thought. *It is uncomfortable to win and face the anger of others.*

After the game, I decided that money was not something I was going to seek. I wanted enough money to live comfortably, but certainly not too much. Otherwise, I would stand out like I had today, and that did not feel good.

Ultimately, I had proved myself right. I knew I was rich, and that I could win all the money. But I also knew it would come at a cost. Unfortunately, I decided I needed to stay small, stay hidden, and stay well liked.

What I did not consciously realize that day was why I felt so wealthy inside – unfortunately, fully understanding that piece of the puzzle would take years.

As I studied *A Course in Miracles* I was introduced to the idea of my spirit being eternal love – whole and pure. This is truly what I had felt as a kid. I knew I was rich beyond belief, but the richness I felt was the wealth of my spirit.

We all come from eternal love as an extension of God. Together, we are God's one son. We can, however, deny this natural inheritance or just be totally oblivious to our origin. If we only look at the physical world and believe we are just our bodies, some of us appear to be poor and lacking.

When we look at the world this way, we are literally making ourselves out to be God. In fact, we are judging that we know more than God. We proclaim poverty by looking around at things, resources, and money and comparing ourselves to others. We look outwards to judge our wealth instead of looking inwards to whether we are richly valued. But no matter what we think, God's love for us never falters or changes. We can either receive our natural inheritance (which is our God-given right), or we can back away and pretend we do not know of this internal wealth.

It is our choice.

As a child, I knew this feeling of deep and profound wealth. I knew I was rich, and nothing on the outside could deter me from this deep knowledge. Things like "The Money Game," however, confused me and entangled me in diversions. Rather than celebrate my inner wealth, for years I thought I needed to hide it. I let myself shrink rather than shine.

Today, I know my inner wealth and rich inheritance is something to embrace and reveal, not something to deny or hide.

We are all internally the same. We are all loved and richly valued for who we truly are at our essence: an eternal, loving, creative spirit. We all come from love, light, and eternal life. When I am in touch with my inner wealth, I can give freely to others. Nothing can take this knowledge from me; it is my divine right and my divine inheritance.

True poverty is poverty of the spirit. You can have nothing (no-things) but still know you are everything! This inner wealth is true wealth. It is the richness of spirit.

Physical money is actually neutral – in essence, money does not have power. It is just pieces of paper or bits of metal. When we understand that money is not real power, but rather our inner spirit, we can step forward without fear. No one can rob you of this wealth. No one can take this wealth from you. It is your natural inheritance to feel abundant, whole, and complete. And, this inner wealth never denies anyone else their wealth – in fact, it is more like a flame that can ignite other flames.

Personally, I have learned that when I am brave enough to stand up, let my light shine and speak my truth, I give others permission to do the same. This inner wealth is what makes everyone richer.

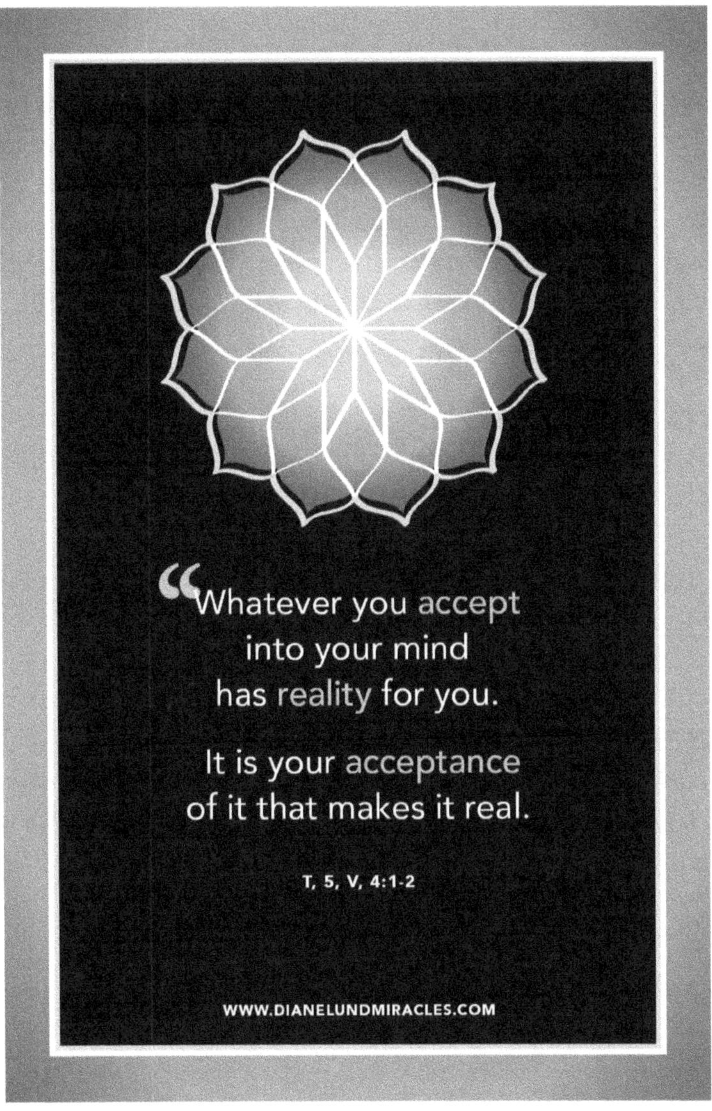

WHAT DOES *A COURSE IN MIRACLES* SAY ABOUT WEALTH?

The Western world often appears dominated by the accumulation of money or wealth. The more money you have, the more you are worth in our society. However, this measuring tool can easily fail us. Remember the economic crisis of 2008? Many people lost their jobs and homes, and they had no idea what had happened to cause it.

At the time, I was a member of an entrepreneurial business group, and we had a mentor who was all about tracking money. I asked him, "How did this crisis happen?" He answered, "I have no idea." Money changes from day to day; it can be worth one amount today and another amount tomorrow.

Money is a game we play. As long as you realize it is just a game, and you can enjoy it, you are fine. The minute you believe the game defines who you truly are, though, you will inevitably lose. You are not your money, and money does not tell you whether you are rich or poor. When you know who you are as an eternal spirit with eternal life and love, you are now internally wealthy – and this wealth only grows when you give it away. It grows because you can only give what, in faith, you know you have. Giving it away and still feeling it inside strengthens you. It proves to you who you truly are, and that the gift of love is truly eternal.

THOSE WHO ATTACK ARE POOR
"Remember that those who attack are poor. Their poverty asks for gifts, not for further impoverishment."
T, 12, III, 3:3-4

POVERTY IS OF THE EGO
"Poverty is of the Ego, and never of God."
T, 12, III, 4:7

THE EGO WANTS TO HAVE THINGS
"The Ego wants to have things for salvation, for possession is its law. Possession for its own sake is the Ego's fundamental creed, a basic cornerstone in the churches it builds to itself. And at its altar it demands you lay all of the things it bids you get, leaving you no joy in them."
T, 13, 10:11-13

IT IS A WORLD OF SCARCITY

"Your Father knoweth that you have need of nothing. In Heaven this is so, for what could you need in eternity? In your world, you do need things. It is a world of scarcity in which you find yourself because you are lacking."

T, 13, 10:2-5

POVERTY IS LACK

"For poverty is lack, and there is but one lack since there is but one need."

T, 12, II, 1:6

THE POOR INVESTED WRONGLY

"The poor are merely those who have invested wrongly, and they are poor indeed! Because they are in need it is given you to help them, since you are among them."

T, 12, II, 1:3

THINK OF THE FREEDOM

"Think of the freedom in the recognition that you are not bound by all the strange and twisted laws you have set up to save you. You really think that you would starve unless you have stacks of green paper strips and piles of metal discs."

W, L76, 3:1-2

GOD'S LAWS FOREVER GIVE AND NEVER TAKE

"There are no laws but God's. Dismiss all foolish magical beliefs today, and hold your mind in silent readiness to hear the Voice that speaks the truth to you. You will be listening to One who says there is no loss under the laws of God. Payment is neither given nor received. Exchange cannot be made; there are no substitutes; and nothing is replaced by something else. God's laws forever give and never take."

W, L76, 9:1-6

PART FOUR

LET'S GET PRACTICAL:
Putting Reverse Thinking
Into Action

*"No one has ever lived who has not experienced
some light and some thing.
No one, therefore, is able to deny truth totally,
even if he thinks he can."*

T, 3, II, 1:7-8

INTRODUCTION

THE RECOGNITION THAT YOU DO NOT UNDERSTAND IS A PREREQUISITE!

"The recognition that you do not understand is a prerequisite for undoing your false ideas.
These exercises are concerned with practice, not with understanding.
You do not need to practice what you already understand.
It would indeed be circular to aim at understanding,
and assume that you have it already."

W, L9, 1:4-7

"It is difficult for the untrained mind to believe that what it seems to picture is not there.
This idea can be quite disturbing, and may meet with active resistance in any number of forms.
Yet that does not preclude applying it.
No more than that is required for these or any other exercises.
Each small step will clear a little of the darkness away, and understanding will finally come to lighten
every corner of the mind that has been cleared of the debris that darkens it."

W, L9, 2:1-5

THE EARTH IS A CLASSROOM

The earth is a classroom where we come to learn. Everything we do here is for our higher good, as it can be used as a tool to teach us about love or about separation and fear.

Ultimately, we decide what we are going to learn at what time. However, the curriculum is always the same for everyone.

You came here to forgive all the illusions you have made up about yourself and others. In reality, you came here to reclaim who you truly are: the light and love of God. But these are simply words that few can hear. In order for these words to mean anything, we need practical experiences. We need to prove it to ourselves.

HERE ARE SOME WAYS YOU CAN START

A. START SIMPLE: Reverse Your Thoughts.

Whenever you think something negative or find yourself feeling uncomfortable, make an effort to focus on what you are thinking. Just try to observe your thought, then turn this thought upside-down. This is the most simple and profound practice.

REVERSE THINKING
"Seek not to change the world.
Choose to change your mind about the world."
T, 21, Introduction, 1:7

If you think, *"I am poor,"*
turn it upside down: *"I am rich."*
Remember that you are rich in your spiritual heritage. You are everything that God is, because you are an extension of God. By looking at life from a spiritual perspective and not just a physical perspective, you can acknowledge God's truth about you and not just your own small opinions of yourself. Let's try another example.

If you think, *"I do not know anything,"*
turn it upside down: *"I do know everything."*
You know everything within your spirit. You are perfect and eternal, and you have access to the knowledge within just like everyone else. However, you cover this up within your mind when you believe you don't know. You then actually do not know, because you yourself are putting up an eternal block to the knowledge. Trust yourself to receive what you already know.

Open up to "what is" within you.

B. GET INSPIRED: Do You Want Weekly Inspiration?

Then consider the following:
- Sign up for Free Monday Miracle Moments Inspirational Cards.
- Watch Monday Miracle Moment Videos about the cards.

People in my study groups love to pull cards with inspirational quotes from *A Course in Miracles*. It seems people always pull the card that addresses a question they have expressed or comments on the evening's reading.

Monday Miracle Moments are an electronic version of pulling an *A Course in Miracles* inspirational card. Trust that the universe will be delivering the message you need to your email each week on Monday morning. The card is laid out beautifully, (an example can be seen on the right) so it can be printed out and put up on your wall to inspire you throughout the week!

In addition, you can request to become a member of the closed Facebook page entitled "Diane Lund's Monday Miracles." There I will post a short video about the weekly inspirational message. I think of it as bite-sized learning, because you can dip your toe into *A Course in Miracles* wisdom without joining a group. To learn more, follow the links below.

SIGN UP
FOR MONDAY MIRACLE MOMENTS
www.bit.ly/mondaymiracles

TO WATCH THE VIDEOS
Become a member of our closed Monday Miracle Moment Group
www.facebook.com/groups/dianelundmiracles/

C. CREATE A STUDY GROUP: Do you want to study with others?

Consider setting up an *A Course in Miracles* study group.

A Course in Miracles is a practical self-study guide. It says:
"This is a course in mind training. All learning involves attention and study at some level."
T, 1, VII, 4:1-2

If you are drawn to study more about *A Course in Miracles*, why not set up your own study group? You do not have to be the teacher – remember, everyone is both teacher and student. All you need is a sincere desire to learn how to improve your life. I am happy for you to use the study group format I have used for years, which you can download from my website.

Go to www.dianelundmiracles.ca
Click on *Free Downloads* on the homepage
Click on *Free Study Group Format*
Download and follow the instructions

D. PRACTICE: Put Reverse Thinking to Work In Your Life.

Here's a SOULution: take one of my online courses! There are three courses based on this book, entitled:
- Life's Big Questions,
- Relationships,
- Work and Career.

Each SOULution course will run for six weeks online. For start dates go to **www.dianelundmiracles.ca**

The format for each of the courses is as follows.
- **READ** the story.
- **DISCUSS** some quotes from *A Course in Miracles* which illustrate the spiritual principle we are studying.
- **EXERCISE** reverse thinking by reviewing the exercises for the week.
- **JOURNAL** about your experience over the week.
- **MEDITATE** to quiet the mind.

In my life, I have found it is always better doing things together. If we want to get to our true home, it is all about embracing each other – all our brothers and sisters. I would be delighted to have you join me in the journey.

Go to www.dianelundmiracles.com
In the navigation bar, click on *Courses*

E. SHARE YOUR MIRACLES: Tell Us About the Miracles in Your Life.

Remember, a miracle is a change in perception – instead of thinking from fear, you change your mind and think from love.

We would love to hear about your miracles! *A Course in Miracles* is a prove-it-to-yourself course. When you practice changing your mind and see remarkable transformations, it always feels good to share. And personally, I find it is always inspiring and enlightening to read other people's miracles.

Join our open facebook page: www.facebook.com/dianelundmiracles/

F. COLLABORATIVE MIRACLES BOOKS: Write Your Miracles Story and Become an Author With Me.

A miracle according to *A Course in Miracles* is a change in perception – from thinking with fear and to thinking from love. We will be creating a series of books where people collaborate to share their miracle stories. If you have a story you would like to share in one of these upcoming books, please go the website to see how you can apply to take. **www.dianelundmiracles/books/collaborative**

I CHOOSE

I choose me, certainly late in life,
but nevertheless, it was at last
a conscious decision not to leave myself out,
or behind, or unfulfilled, or empty,
waiting for others to give me a drink.
No, it was bold!
Foot first, head up, fully awake.
A choice, long overdue
yet always suspected,
hinted at between conversations
and whispered sounds.
It showed itself in glints of light,
like a firefly
ready to write
my name,
finally, in light.

Rev. Diane C. Lund

Come Join Me.
Write Your Name In Light
Within our Spiritual Community.

Come Home To Love.

"You know when you have ceased to ask questions."
T, 3, III, 2:11

IN GRATITUDE

There are always so many people to thank in the creation of a book. Influence Publishing and Julie Salisbury, who guided my writing process and held my feet to the fire so I would finish this book. Thank you for your friendship, flexibility and many laughs.

Thank you to the many women who supported me through the process of creating this book.
- The women in my "Inspire-A-Book" class, who asked me to write my fourth book first!
- The ladies from the Turks and Caicos writing retreat
- The women from the Puerto Vallarta writing retreat
- The women from my France writing retreat
- The women in my Friday Night Author Group
- The women in my Mexico retreat

To my co-creators in the book, *WOW: Woman of Worth: Power. Passion. Purpose.* In that book, fifteen empowered entrepreneurs share success stories with soul, and I am a contributing author. My word for that year was co-creation, and you made that word come alive.

To my *A Course In Miracles* study groups throughout the decades. So many wonderful people. Together we are both teachers and students. Sharing the journey home to God is part of my Happy Dream. Thank you for being there on Monday nights to share your hearts and souls. To the Miracles Minister's Group for our year of devotion together to God.

To the people in my Get-it-Done Mastermind Group for stepping out together. Tamara Monosoff, thank you for your never-ending enthusiastic ideas and loving support!

My proofreaders Lee, Reverend Lisa Windsor, and Melanie Tremblay. Thank you Lisa for proofreading the initial document, and for your wise commentary and leadership in our Ministry Training Program. Your support means the world to me. Thank you to Danielle Anderson for the final edit, Flora Gordon for the design and Sharon McKenzie for working through each revision. Thank you to Allison Barton Youssef at Soulography for the photograph used on the book cover.

Thank you to all my dear friends and family, who have believed in me and loved me through the process of writing this book – especially my sisters Jennifer Hamner and Lori Phillips, my mother May Lund (who is at the centre of many of my life stories), and my dear friends Martha Markus and Lynn Sumida who have held my hand and my heart through many of my life stories.

Last but never least, to my husband Dr. Brian O'Connor for loving and supporting me all-ways. You rock! Love is the greatest gift. Pass it on.

I WOULD LOVE TO HEAR FROM YOU!

If you enjoyed reading this book, it would mean a lot to me if you left a review on Amazon.

LEARN MORE ABOUT REVEREND DIANE C. LUND

CREATIVE PORTFOLIO
- www.creativewonders.ca

FACEBOOK
- www.facebook.com/creativewondersinc

LINKED-IN
- www.linkedin.com/in/dianelund/

PINTEREST
- www.pinterest.ca/seeourwonders/

E-BOOK
Ready Aim Fire: They Keys To Unlocking Business Creativity
- www.bit.ly/readyaimfirePDF

AWARDS
- **2019 International Silver Award** – Most Original Calendar World Calendar Awards - Multifaith Calendar 2019: Coming Together: Exploring New Connections
- **2017 International Silver Summit Award** - Online Marketing Effectiveness for Vancouver's North Shore Tourism campaign
- **2017 The Visioneers International Network** - Lifetime Achievement Award for Innovation and Entrepreneurship
- **2017 International Bronze Summit Creative Award** - Print Speciality
- **2017 International Judges Finalist Summit Creative Award** - Print
- **Chamber of Commerce Business Excellence Award for Best Business** - Creative Wonders Communications
- **Ethics in Actions Award** - Community Care. For "exceeding the vast majority of the CBSR (Canadian Business for Social Responsibility) guidelines, and showing huge heart by giving an unheard of 50% of profits or 15% of revenues to their community in support of building a better world." – N. Bradshaw Founder CBSR